Professional Rails Testing

Jason Swett

ii

Contents

Acknowledgements

First and most importantly I want to thank my beautiful and loving wife, Niki, for supporting all my craziness over the years. I also want to thank my sons, Elliott and Oliver, for tolerating their father working so much.

I'd also like to thank (in alphabetical order) Adrian Marin, Alex Hillman, Amanda Perino, Amy Hoy, Andrew Atkinson, Andrew Katz, Andrew Mason, Andy Croll, Brendan Buckingham, Chris Oliver, Daniel Westendorf, David Heinemeier Hansson, Drew Bragg, Ernesto Tagwerker, Freedom Dumlao, Harry Sohie, Helmut Kobler, Irina Nazarova, James Couball, Jason Charnes, Jeremy Smith, Jonathan Bennett, Jonathan Gennick, Karl McCollester, Lucian Ghinda, Mark Shead, Martin Lee, Nate Berkopec, Neeraj Singh, Nick Schwaderer, Obie Fernandez, Patrick Foley, Peter Cai, Rick Smoke, Robby Russell, Rob Zolkos, Ryan Frisch, Sanjit Joseph, Todd Siegel, Tom Henrik Aadland, Tom Rossi, Trae Robrock, and Vladimir Dementyev.

Chapter 1

Introduction

Testing is a bit like flossing. Everybody agrees it's a good idea, everybody knows they should do it, yet hardly anyone does it. Testing also shares a reputation with flossing your teeth as being an unpleasant chore. Or, at the very best, it's merely boring.

Actually, testing need be neither unpleasant nor boring. In fact, if you allow yourself to be brainwashed by this book as I hope you will, you'll not only enjoy testing but wonder how you ever tolerated the pain of writing software *without* tests. My aspiration with this book is to convert you to an entirely different way of looking at programming, a mindset that puts testing at the center of all your programming activities.

1.1   Who this book is for

This book is for developers of all levels of experience with automated testing. If you're an absolute beginner, my hope is that this book will frame testing for you in a way that makes sense to your beginner's perspective. If you're already quite experienced with testing, I like to think that this book will show you some new ideas that you haven't yet considered.

1.2   What to expect from this book

Learning testing is hard. Really hard. Making testing a habitual part of your development workflow can take years. I don't expect that anyone will be able to read this book and suddenly gain many new capabilities. I'll be happy if this book merely helps open your eyes to some new ideas and look at testing and programming in a different way than you did before.

If you want to truly commit yourself to learning testing and spend the next few years of your career building your testing skills, I think this book can help you greatly along your journey, although you should recognize that learning testing will unavoidably take a lot of time and a lot of work.

1.3   Will we use RSpec or Minitest?

In the Rails community, the two dominant test frameworks are RSpec and Minitest. Since it would not have been practical for me to show both an RSpec example and a Minitest example every time I needed to show some test code, I had to pick one or the other. I chose to go with RSpec. I made this choice not because I have a personal preference for RSpec (although I do) but because, given that most commercial Rails projects use RSpec, it's overwhelmingly more likely that you, dear reader, will have to work with RSpec at your job than with Minitest.

1.4   Want more help with testing?

I hope, of course, that this book is a great help to you on its own. But if you want to get even more assistance as you learn testing and apply it to your production applications, I offer several additional ways of getting help.

1. **Online meetup.** As of this writing, I run a twice-weekly online meeting called the Code with Jason Meetup. These meetings usually consist of a live coding session, a presentation by yours truly, a mentorship session or simply a casual discussion about programming. If you'd like to attend the Code with Jason Meetup, you can sign up at
   `https://www.codewithjason.com/meetup`.

2. **Free mentorship.** Sometimes it helps to get some one-on-one help from an experienced person. That's exactly what I offer in my free mentorship program. The way the mentorship program works is that 1) you apply for membership, 2) I get back to you about scheduling, and then 3) we have a mentorship session during one of the Code with Jason Meetup sessions.
   `https://www.codewithjason.com/free-mentorship`.

3. **Consulting/coaching/teaching.** If you're a CTO or engineering manager, you might want help leveling up your teams skills, or you might want coaching as to how you yourself can get your team to practice testing the way you would like them to. If you'd like to learn about how I can help you, you can get more information at
   `http://www.codewithjason.com/consulting`. Or if you'd like to cut to the chase you can just email me directly at `jason@codewithjason.com`.

4. **Email newsletter.** If you like, you can join a few thousand of your fellow Rails developers and get testing tips (and other programming tips) in your

email inbox about once a week. The best way to get on the list is to go to `https://www.codewithjason.com/rails-testing-guide` and sign up to get my *Beginner's Guide to Rails Testing*, which will also automatically put you on my email list.

5. **Snail mail newsletter.** Believe it or not, you can also get mail from me in your actual physical mailbox. Once a month I send a programming newsletter called *Nonsense Monthly*. For a small annual fee, you can sign up to receive the newsletter by visiting
`https://www.codewithjason.com/snail-mail-newsletter`.

With those things out of the way, we may now let the brainwashing begin.

Part I

Principles

Chapter 2

Tests as specifications

If you take away only one lesson from this book, I hope it's the lesson that you shouldn't think of tests as *verifications* but rather as *specifications*. The aim of testing isn't to "make sure the code worked" but rather to enforce that the code *behaves as specified*. It's a subtle difference but an important one.

If you go to a squirt gun factory, for example, you can grab any individual squirt gun off of the end of the line. You may perform any number of tests on the squirt gun and observe the result. As you do this, you can have one of two questions in your head:

1. Does *this individual squirt gun* function properly, or is it defective?

2. Does the *manufacturing system* behave properly? That is, does it output a squirt gun that meets its *design specifications*, or does the manufacturing system behave incorrectly, and produce squirt guns that doesn't match their specifications?

In the first scenario, the subject of scrutiny is the individual artifact. In the second, it's the system that produces the artifact. In both cases, the tests are being performed on the same physical object, an individual squirt gun. The difference is the purpose for which the tests are being carried out.

Many Rails tests belie that the author was thinking in a verification mindset rather than a specification mindset. The test cases are expressed in terms of *capabilities* rather than *scenarios*.

The assertions of a verification-style test suite might include, for example:

- The user can update their email address

- The user can sign in

- The user can reset their password

Conversely, the assertions of a specification-style test suite might include the following:

- When the user signs in with valid credentials, the dashboard page is shown

- When the user attempts to sign in with invalid credentials, an error message is shown

Notice how the specification-style assertions speak in terms of scenarios rather than capabilities.

2.1   What is a specification?

A specification is **a statement of how some aspect of a software product should behave**. Let's take the sign-in example a bit further.

1. **Scenario**: when a user enters a valid email address and password combination into the email and password fields, then clicks 'Sign In'

   a. **Expectation**: the user's dashboard page is shown.

2. **Scenario**: when a user enters a valid email address into the email field but an invalid password, then clicks 'Sign In'

   a. **Expectation**: an error message appears that says "Unable to sign in."

   b. **Expectation**: the user's dashboard page is *not* shown.

3. **Scenario**: when a user leaves the username and password fields blank

   a. **Expectation**: an error message appears that says "Email can't be left blank"

   b. **Expectation**: an error message appears that says "Password can't be left blank"

   c. **Expectation**: the user's dashboard page is *not* shown.

I want to note carefully that God has not descended to earth to decree a single correct way of expressing specifications. This is just a style that I happen to think makes sense. "Under such-and-such scenario, we expect such-and-such behavior." Soon we'll see how such specifications can be neatly mapped onto automated tests.

2.2 Example: expression parser

Common features like sign-in pages are easy to discuss because they're so familiar. Unfortunately, when it comes to real test code, features like this don't make the best examples. Testing a sign-in page for a real Rails application would involve creating test users in the database, using tools to manipulate the browser, and other distractions that would obscure the lessons I want to share in this chapter. We'll get into full-stack testing later but not now.

Because I want to focus as much as possible on testing *principles* rather than testing *tools*, the example program we're going to build in this section will not be a Rails application or even a web application at all. Instead it will be a pure Ruby program with which we interact with using only the command line.

The program will parse a mathematical expression into its constituent parts. The expression 2x + 5 for example would get split into two parts, 2x and 5. And since 2x is itself an expression that has two parts, it would get split into 2 and x.

How shall we tackle this problem? When parsing an expression into a tree, each node can be expressed as having an operator as its root, and then a left child node and a right child node. Each child node can be either another tree with an operator at its root or just a value, a "leaf node". Here is, for example, the tree that we would get from the expression 2x + 5.

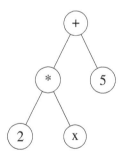

What about a more complicated expression like, for example, 3x^2 + 5x + 1? This expression has three terms, so it may appear not to fit our plan of having exactly two children per node. But we can take care of this issue by grouping the last two terms with parentheses, turning the two terms into a single expression, like this: 3x^2 + (5x + 1). Now no operator has more than two operands. Here's what this expression would look like represented as a tree.

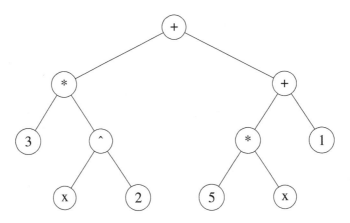

How might we interact with our command-line expression-parsing program? One possible design is that we could pass as an argument a single expression enclosed in a string. In response we're shown the expression represented as a crude tree. Here's how it might look to use the program.

```
$ ruby parser.rb "2x + 5"
+
..*
....2
....x
..5

$ ruby parser.rb "3x^2 + (5x + 1)"
+
..*
....3
....^
......x
......2
..+
....*
......5
......x
....1
```

Now that we have a high-level overview of the program's behavior, let's come up with some specific specifications.

2.2.1 Expression parser specifications

We still have a little bit more work to do regarding our approach. Where exactly are we going to start?

We can go from the bottom up. Instead of asking "how can we parse an entire expression?" let's ask "how can we parse a single term?" Another way of putting that, since every term itself is also an expression, is "how can we parse a single-term expression?"

For the moment let's only concern ourselves with specifications related to parsing one-term expressions. Once we've made some progress in that area maybe we can set our ambitions higher. Here are some specifications we could use.

1. **Scenario**: when the expression involves multiplication with an explicit operator (example: 2*x)

    a. **Expectation**: the root of the expression is the multiplication operator. If for example the expression is 2*x, the parsed expression's root is *.

    b. **Expectation**: the left child is the first operand. If for example the expression is 2*x, the parsed expression's first child is 2.

    c. **Expectation**: the right child is the second operand. If for example the expression is 2*x, the parsed expression's second child is x.

2. **Scenario**: when the expression involves multiplication without an explicit operator (example: 2x)

    a. **Expectation**: the root of the expression is the multiplication operator. If for example the expression is 2x, the parsed expression's root is *.

    b. **Expectation**: the left child is the first operand. If for example the expression is 2x, the parsed expression's left child is 2.

    c. **Expectation**: the right child is the second operand. If for example the expression is 2x, the parsed expression's right child is x.

3. **Scenario**: the expression involves division (example: x/3)

    a. **Expectation**: the root of the expression is the division operator. If for example the expression is x/3, the parsed expression's root is /.

    b. **Expectation**: the left child is the first operand. If for example the expression is x/3, the parsed expression's left child is x.

    c. **Expectation**: the right child is the second operand. If for example the expression is x/3, the parsed expression's right child is 3.

4. **Scenario**: when the expression is a constant (example: 5)

    a. **Expectation**: the root of the expression is the constant itself. For example, if the constant is 5, the parsed expression's root is 5.

    b. **Expectation**: the expression's left child is empty.

    c. **Expectation**: the expression's right child is empty.

How do we translate these specifications into tests?

2.3   How to translate specifications into working tests

Many developers get "writer's block" when trying to write tests. This is often a symptom of trying to write tests before any concrete specifications have been decided. The writer's block problem is also often exacerbated by not having a repeatable process to use when translating specifications into tests. Furthermore, developers often unconciously try to think about multiple things at once and therefore make progress on none of them.

Assuming that sound specifications have already been developed, here's a process that can be used to turn the specifications into tests. The idea with each step is to expend as little mental energy as possible.

1. **Filename.** When you write a test, it obviously has to get saved somewhere on the filesystem. The first decision to be made when writing a test is what to name the file and in what folder to put it. I recommend initially giving the test the "dumbest" name you can think of, even if that means naming it something like `thing_spec.rb`. We can always change our mind later. Later our test file will actually have some tests in it, and those tests can give us some clarity on what the file is all about and how it should be named.

2. **Boilerplate.** Every test is going to have some amount of boilerplate: the code that goes at the top that's roughly the same for every test. Here's an example.

   ```
   # The test description can be a class name
   RSpec.describe ExpressionParser do
   end

   # or an abritrary string
   RSpec.describe "expression parser" do
   end
   ```

   Since this step is more or less the same for every single test, we can get it out of the way without having to think much about the test's actual contents. The only thing we'll have to think of is a high-level description. Just like with the filename, we don't have to get this right on the first try. We can fill in the boilerplate with something as vague as e.g. `RSpec.describe "stuff"` and then fill it in with something better later. A fitting description for the test will become more obvious after some test cases are written.

3. **Specification in prose.** We can think of writing a test as having two layers: 1) deciding what the test is going to do and 2) figuring out the syntax to get the test to do it. If we separate these two jobs, testing is easier. If we mix them, testing is harder. I recommend starting by putting comments inside the test file describing what you want the test to be. If you've developed your

specifications before writing your tests then this step is often trivial: you can just copy/paste the specification into the test as a comment. Once the "what" of the test is out of your mind and onto the screen, you can clear your "mental RAM" and focus entirely on the "how".

4. **Scenarios.** In the case of our expression parser, the scenarios we came up with included things like "multiplication with explicit operator" and "multiplication with implicit operator". We can divide the test we're writing into sections based on these scenarios.

5. **Expectations.** Once the scenarios are in place we can fill them in with expectations. For example, under the "multiplication with explicit operator" scenario we would place the "it has a root of *" expectation.

6. **Setup, exercise and assertion.** Many tests follow a pattern of setup, exercise and assertion, also known by the alliterative mnemonic *arrange, act, assert*. These three phases are all sufficiently involved that we'll be discussing each in depth in later chapters.

Now that we've discussed these steps in the abstract, let's apply them to the specifications for our expression parser.

2.4   Tests for the expression parser program

In this section we'll go through each of our expression parser scenarios individually, and for each scenario we'll go through each expectation. We won't go through the entirety of the expression parser specifications, only enough to give you a feel for the process.

2.4.1   Tests for expression root

First we'll go through the scenario of a multiplication expression with an explicit operator, and the expectation that the parsed expression's root node will be *. To save you some page flipping, here's the first expectation of the first scenario.

1. **Scenario**: when the expression involves multiplication with an explicit operator (example: 2*x)

    a. **Expectation**: the root of the expression is the multiplication operator. If for example the expression is 2*x, the parsed expression's root is *.

In order to implement this test, we can follow the steps from the beginning of section the previous section, starting with the name of the test file.

Filename

Since we've been calling our program a "expression parser" thus far, we can name
our test file `expression_parser_spec.rb`. We'll surely want to change the name
to something more specific later, but no need to waste brainpower on that now.

Boilerplate

Next we can address the test's boilerplate. Again, in the spirit of conserving brainpower, we'll just give the test a tentative description of "expression parser".

```
# expression_parser_spec.rb

RSpec.describe "expression parser" do
end
```

It's very likely that a more fitting name will easily occur to us later, once the
file is populated with some tests.

Specification in prose

The smallest, easiest next step we can take is to simply restate our specification in
the form of a comment. Let's paste our original specification verbatim into the test.

```
RSpec.describe "expression parser" do
  # Scenario: when the expression involves multiplication
  # with an explicit operator (example: 2*x)
  #
  # Expectation: the root of the expression is the
  # multiplication operator. If for example the expression
  # is 2*x, the parsed expression's root is *.
end
```

Having completed the baby step of bringing the specifications into the test file
as comments, we can now turn the comments into working code bit-by-bit.

Scenarios and expectations

We can map our scenario, "the expression involves multiplication with an explicit
operator", to a `context` block, and our expectation, "it assigns the multiplication
operator to the root", to an `it` block.

```
RSpec.describe "expression parser" do
  context "the expression involves multiplication with" \
    "an explicit operator" do
    it "assigns the multiplication operator to the root" do
    end
```

```
  end
end
```

Now that we have the complete "shell" of the test in place, we can write the part of the test that actually performs the assertion. When we do this, we can practice "outside-in" code design, where we first imagine the code we wish existed, and then add the supporting code to make it actually work.

Setup, exercise and assertion

Before we start writing code let's pause and think for a moment. What might a good API for our expression parser look like? Since an expression can be represented as a tree with a root, a left child and a right child, maybe we can conceive of an `Expression` object with attributes called `root`, `left_child` and `right_child`. We can create an instance of `Expression` and assert that its root attribute is equal to *.

We still have one more thing to think about. If our program is supposed to be an expression *parser* that parses an expression from a string, how do we get from the string to the `Expression` object whose `root` we check? Perhaps we can have a class method called, say, `parse`, which takes a string and returns an instance of `Expression`.

```
RSpec.describe "expression parser" do
  context "the expression involves multiplication with" \
    "an explicit operator" do
    it "assigns the multiplication operator to the root" do
      expression = Expression.parse("2*x")
      expect(expression.root).to eq("*")
    end
  end
end
```

Now our test is complete enough that we could, in principle, run the test and then write the code to make it pass. But this chapter is limited to the question of how to convert a specification into test code, not the complete test-driven development process. We'll cover the rest in another chapter.

2.4.2 Tests for left child

Now that we have a test for root we can write a test for our next expectation under the "multiplication with explicit operator" scenario, the expectation that the first operand of the expression gets assigned to its left child.

For convenience, here again is the specification for left child.

1. **Scenario**: when the expression involves multiplication with an explicit operator (example: 2*x)

b. **Expectation**: the left child is the first operand. If for example the expression is 2*x, the parsed expression's first child is 2.

Specification in prose

Like before, we'll begin by simply copy/pasting the text of the specification into the test. (In the following code examples we'll omit the root tests so they don't distract us.)

```
RSpec.describe "expression parser" do
  # Scenario: when the expression involves multiplication
  # with an explicit operator (example: 2*x)
  #
  # Expectation: the left child is the first operand. If
  # for example the expression is 2*x, the parsed
  # expression's first child is 2.
end
```

Scenario and expectation

Also like last time, we'll map the scenario onto a *context* block and the expectation onto an *it* block.

```
RSpec.describe "expression parser" do
  context "the expression involves multiplication with" \
    "an explicit operator" do
    it "assigns the first operand to the left child" do
    end
  end
end
```

Now let's fill in the example with some code.

Setup, exercise and assertion

Since in the previous test we invented the idea of an `Expression` object we can use the same concept in this test.

```
RSpec.describe "expression parser" do
  context "the expression involves multiplication with" \
    "an explicit operator" do
    it "assigns the first operand to the left child" do
      expression = Expression.parse("2*x")
      expect(expression.left_child).to eq(2)
    end
  end
end
```

The only difference between the last test and this one is that in the last test we were asserting that the root is * whereas here we're asserting that left_child is 2.

All of the tests together

Here are the two explicit multiplication operator tests we've written so far, shown together.

```
RSpec.describe "expression parser" do
  context "the expression involves multiplication with" \
    "an explicit operator" do
    it "assigns the multiplication operator to the root" do
      expression = Expression.parse("2*x")
      expect(expression.root).to eq("*")
    end

    it "assigns the first operand to the left child" do
      expression = Expression.parse("2*x")
      expect(expression.left_child).to eq(2)
    end
  end
end
```

Lastly, let's add some tests for right child.

2.4.3   Tests for right child

Here's the expectation for right child.

1. **Scenario**: when the expression involves multiplication with an explicit operator (example: 2*x)

    c. **Expectation**: the right child is the second operand. If for example the expression is 2*x, the parsed expression's first child is x.

Since you've already seen the process a couple of times now, we can skip straight to the finished test. Here it is along with the other two tests we wrote.

```
RSpec.describe "expression parser" do
  context "the expression involves multiplication with" \
    "an explicit operator" do
    it "assigns the multiplication operator to the root" do
      expression = Expression.parse("2*x")
      expect(expression.root).to eq("*")
    end

    it "assigns the first operand to the left child" do
```

```
      expression = Expression.parse("2*x")
      expect(expression.left_child).to eq(2)
    end

    it "assigns the second operand to the right child" do
      expression = Expression.parse("2*x")
      expect(expression.right_child).to eq("x")
    end
  end
end
```

These tests cover all three expectations for the scenario in which the expression contains an explicit multiplication operator, like the expression 2*x. Now let's address the scenario where, as in the expression 2x for example, the multiplication operator is implicit.

2.4.4   Next scenario: multiplication without explicit operator

   2. **Scenario**: when the expression involves multiplication without an explicit operator (example: 2x)

      a. **Expectation**: the root of the expression is the multiplication operator. If for example the expression is 2x, the parsed expression's root is *.

      b. **Expectation**: the left child is the first operand. If for example the expression is 2x, the parsed expression's left child is 2.

      c. **Expectation**: the right child is the second operand. If for example the expression is 2x, the parsed expression's right child is x.

This time we'll completely skip the test-writing steps and go straight to the finished tests.

```
RSpec.describe "expression parser" do
  context "the expression involves multiplication without" \
          "an explicit operator" do
    it "assigns the multiplication operator to the root" do
      expression = Expression.parse("2x")
      expect(expression.root).to eq("*")
    end

    it "assigns the first operand to the left child" do
      expression = Expression.parse("2x")
      expect(expression.left_child).to eq(2)
    end

    it "assigns the second operand to the right child" do
      expression = Expression.parse("2x")
```

```
      expect(expression.right_child).to eq("x")
    end
  end
end
```

When we start the software development process with detailed specifications for the behavior we want, it forces us to decide what we want to do before we attempt to do it. When we write our tests in a way that reflects the specifications we've come up with, it makes it easier to look at the tests and understand the system's behavior.

Chapter 3

Test-driven development

All code is an artifact of a coding process. A good process, with clear thinking and good habits behind it, will tend to produce good code. A poor process, with muddy thinking and bad habits behind it, will tend to produce poor code.

Same with tests. Test code is just an artifact. The part that really matters is the test-writing process.

3.1   What is test-driven development?

Most definitions of test-driven development (TDD) equate the practice to something called the *red/green/refactor* loop, in which a failing test is written prior to any code, then code is written to make the test pass, and then some refactoring is performed. In Kent Beck's *Test-Driven Development: By Example*, the red/green/refactor loop is described as follows:

1. Red—Write a little test that doesn't work, and perhaps doesn't even compile at first.

2. Green—Make the test work quickly, committing whatever sins necessary in the process.

3. Refactor—Eliminate all of the duplication created in merely getting the test to work.

Even though most TDD definitions include red/green/refactor, what is unfortunately missing from most of these definitions is *why* TDD is done the way it is. Let's address that now.

3.1.1   Red: the failing test

Why does the test-driven development process begin with a failing test? There are multiple reasons. One is because, if we perform the work in the order of 1) writing the test and then 2) writing the code to satisfy the test, then we are 1) deciding what to do and then 2) doing it. Remember that a test is an executable specification. When we write the test first, we're starting with the specification and then writing the code to fulfill the specification. If it seems funny to start with a failing test, maybe it seems a little bit less weird to think of it as first specifying what we want to do and then, secondly, doing it. How could it be any other way?

Starting with a failing test also allows us to test the validity of our test. It's surprisingly easy to devise a test which, for example, always gives a false positive, or tests something that's not exactly what you intended to target. Running the test before we've written the code to satisfy it gives us a chance to verify that the test fails when its requirements are not fulfilled, and fails in exactly the way we expect it to fail. Unless the test we're starting with is valid, the whole endeavor is moot.

3.1.2   Green: making the test pass

The reasoning behind this step is exactly as straightforward as it sounds. Once we have a valid test, all we need to do is write the code to make it pass and then we have a working feature. But what exactly did Kent Beck mean about the "sins"?

The point of this is to separate the work of (to quote Mr. Beck again) "making it work" and "making it right". If we try to make the code meet its functional requirements while *also* trying to make the code as elegant as it can be, we're making life harder on ourselves than it needs to be. Thanks to our tests, we're free to make the code as crappy as we want on the first pass. Our tests will protect us from regressions when we go back and make the code tidy.

Part of the "green" step is to write just enough code to make the test pass and no more. Why is this? Part of the reason is to avoid coding *speculatively*. Speculative coding is when we add code without sufficient evidence that it's needed. Speculative coding also incurs a cost (since all code has a carrying cost) without being sufficiently sure that there will be a return on investment for the cost.

Perhaps more important, writing only enough code to make the test pass results in all our system's behavior being covered by a test. If everything in the system is covered by a test, we can refactor the system's code as much as we want without too much fear that our refactoring will introduce regressions. Full test coverage doesn't provide an *absolute guarantee* that refactorings won't introduce regressions, it merely provides a high degree of well-justified confidence.

There's actually a certain aspect of the generally-accepted TDD wisdom that I think has some room for improvement. When I'm practicing the "green" step of TDD, I don't write just enough code to make the test pass. I write just enough code *to make the current failure message go away*. Even if we make the tests as small and granular as they can be, going from a freshly failing test all the way to a passing state often requires a non-trivial amount of thinking and coding. It can be a relatively large leap. It's often a big enough leap to leave room for speculative coding. To give myself less room for speculative coding. If I write only enough code to make the current failure message go away instead of writing enough code to make the test pass, it gives me a lot less room to code speculatively.

3.1.3 Refactor: cleaning up the mess

It may be self-evident, but the reason for the "refactor" step is to keep our code in a reasonably tidy and understandable state. It should be noted that the refactor step is optional. Not all code changes call for a refactoring. I personally also find that "I just got done writing a test" is not the only event or even necessarily the main event that prompts me to perform refactoring.

You'll never have a clearer understanding of a piece of code than just after you finish writing it. After all, you've been actively working on the problem that the code solves, and all the details of the problem will be loaded into your short-term memory. It's for this reason that right after you finish writing a piece of code is sometimes the *worst* time to try to refactor it.

Once I've fixed my most embarrassing sins, I usually hold off on any further refactorings. I prefer to give myself enough time to forget about the problem area. The next time I need to work with the code in this area, any shortcomings in my code's understandability will be painfully obvious. Then, instead of refactoring speculatively, I can refactor as to address the exact pain I'm feeling. I don't have to wonder if the investment I'm making in refactoring will have a payoff. The friction my bad code poses to the work I need to do is hard evidence that it will.

3.2 Why practice TDD?

Since you're reading this book, maybe you're already sold on TDD. Even so, here are some of the benefits of the practice. Even if you've been practicing TDD for a long time, some of these benefits may be new to you, or may be viewed from a slightly different angle than what you've seen before.

3.2.1 Speed and productivity

To me, the main reason for practicing TDD (or writing clean code, or following any good programming practice for that matter) is to go faster and be more productive. Some people are put off by this idea, as if my goal is to be an overworked slave to capitalism or something like that. It's not about that at all. I simply want to decrease the ratio of effort invested to value produced. If I have to be at work all day every day no matter what, why would I not want to get more done for equal or lesser effort?

Some might be surprised that I consider coding *with* TDD to be faster than coding *without* TDD. Doesn't it take extra time to write tests? Yes, if you're just getting started with TDD, then adding testing to your workflow is going to introduce friction. But if, like me, your testing abilities are sufficiently strong that writing tests is easy and fun, then TDD on balance is a great net gain. Remember that skipping testing altogether is not an option. It's just a choice of whether your tests are performed manually or automatically. And given that full-system regression tests need to be performed over and over, which approach do you think is faster?

3.2.2   Better design

In order for a piece of code to be tested, it has to be executed, which means that any of its hard dependencies will have be involved in the test as well. Since test-driven development begins with a test, any piece of code written to satisfy the test will be, by necessity, testable, meaning that the code will not have any overly cumbersome dependencies. Test-driven development encourages modular, loosely-coupled design.

In addition to being easy to test, it so happens that modular, loosely-coupled entities also test to be easy to understand and easy to change.

Strictly speaking, it's not necessary to write the tests before the application code in order to achieve loose coupling and modularity. You could write the code, then try to write the tests and refactor the code to make it loosely-coupled enough to be testable. But in general I think it's more efficient just to write the tests first.

3.2.3   Less mental effort

On account of my habit of test-driven development, I occasionally find myself accused of being disciplined. This is very untrue. I'm as lazy as they come.

I think the reason that people think writing tests requires discipline is they haven't yet achieved fluency with testing tools and habits. For them, writing tests is a chore. They imagine that perhaps for me it's a chore as well, I just have enough discipline to carry through with the chore. No, it's just that testing has become such a deeply ingrained part of my workflow that I don't know any other way.

3.2.4   More enjoyable workflow

In a way, it's smart to be lazy. But once in a while I get truly lazy—the stupid kind, not the smart kind. Sometimes I'll slap together a side project just for fun and I'll neglect to write tests, out of a desire to go "fast". But it only takes a matter of hours before my poor judgment comes back to bite me. Inevitably, I'll make some logical error and build a bug into my program. If I had had a thorough suite of tests for my program, I probably wouldn't have introduced the bug in the first place, and if I had, I would have known exactly where the bug does *not* lie because my passing tests would give me evidence of all the parts of my program that are working correctly. The diagnosis process would have been relatively easy. But in the absence of tests,

I'm forced to do a really tedious and annoying manual analysis of the code to try to figure out where the bug lies. It can be quite frustrating.

When coding with tests, everything that works will *stay* working. And if a new change breaks previously-working code, you can get notified immediately so that you can modify your breaking change or simply blow it away and try again a different way.

3.2.5 Fewer bugs

TDD tends to yield software with fewer bugs. There are two reasons for this: an intuitive reason and less obvious one. The intuitive reason why tests prevent bugs is that tests catch bugs before they ever reach production.

The less obvious reason is that, because good test coverage allows liberal refactoring, the design of the project as a whole can be kept in a cleaner and more easily understandable state. Just as a dirty, messy kitchen provides a hospitable environment in which pests can thrive, a sloppy, confusing codebase provides a hospitable environment in which bugs can thrive. A tidy codebase has the opposite effect.

3.2.6 Documentation

As we saw in the previous chapter, tests, when written a certain way, can serve as documentation for a system's behavior. Actually, tests are about the most authoritative possible kind of documentation, since they're physically tied to the system's behavior. In fact, tests are an even more authoritative source of truth for a system's behavior than the system's application code. Application code merely shows what the system's current behavior *is*. Tests show what the system's behavior *should* be.

Soon we'll get into specific TDD methodology. But first, in order for us to better understand the reasons we're doing what we're doing, I want to talk about the principle of *feedback loops*.

3.3 Feedback loops

Because of how complicated computer programs tend to be with respect to human brainpower, we can't work out their behavior in our heads. In order to be certain that a program's behavior matches our expectations, we have to empirically test it, by using either manual or automated tests.

Often, when testing, we'll find that the program's behavior differs from our expectations and we have to make a correction to the code. If after every change we can test our program completely and make any corrections needed so that our program's behavior matches our expectations, then in general our programming work can go quite smoothly, since at no point do we ever get too far off course.

Sadly, not everyone is familiar with this way of working, and their programming work does not go so smoothly. Instead of getting constant feedback on their program's behavior, many developers try to write entire methods or features without even checking for correctness until the piece of code is fully written. By this point the code's behavior has often diverged significantly from what the programmer intended. And since so much code has been written since the last check, it can be very unclear where exactly the problem might lie.

Coding in feedback loops is a process of predicting, testing, correcting, and then predicting, testing and correcting again. We predict that a piece of code we write will behave a certain way, then we perform a test to see if our prediction was right. If our prediction was wrong, then we make corrections to the code and repeat the loop until reality matches our prediction. When the code's behavior does match our prediction, we start the loop again with a new prediction.

Let's now take a more detailed look at the feedback loop process.

3.3.1   How to code in feedback loops

Here's a more precise description of what such a feedback loop might look like. First we'll look at the high-level steps, then we'll go over each step in detail. As you're reading, keep in mind that none of this process has to have anything to do with automated testing. In fact, whenever you see the word "test", think of a manual test, not an automated test.

1. Specify an objective

2. Devise a test that can be performed to see if #1 is done

3. Perform the test devised in step 2

4. Do some work toward the objective (write a line of code)

5. Repeat steps 3 and 4 until the test passes

6. Repeat from step 1 with a new objective

Let's go over these steps individually in detail.

Specify an objective

Remember that tests are specifications. Any attempt at writing a piece of code must start with a sufficiently specific idea of what behavior the code will achieve.

Devise a test that can be performed to see if #1 is done

We saw in the previous chapter how to turn specifications into tests. Remember that a test can be devised by translating a specification into a scenario and a description of exactly what behavior we expect under that scenario. (And remember that a single specification often calls for multiple tests.)

Perform the test devised in step 2

What's the point of performing a test at a stage where we expect it to fail? The point is to test the validity of the test itself. If the test passes when it ought to fail, our test needs adjustment.

The act of testing the test is not an academic exercise or a formality. It's surprisingly easy to accidentally devise an invalid test.

Do some work toward the objective (write a line of code)

In addition to proving the validity of your test, performing the test when you know it will fail will give you a clue as to the nature of the gap between the desired behavior and the current behavior. Based on the test failure, which may be an error message or a more graceful sort of failure, you can write a line of code to try to make the failure go away. (There's nothing special about *one* line of code specifically. The point is to work in very small changes.)

Note carefully that we're not writing enough code to make the test pass, we're only writing enough code to make the current failure message go away. There are two reasons for this. The first is that writing only enough code to make the failure go away helps us to avoid coding *speculatively*. Speculative coding is when we add code before we're really sure it's needed. It often results in code that's buggy, overcomplicated or superfluous. The opposite of speculative coding is when we make each new piece of code earn its keep by demonstrating, via performing a test, that the piece of code gets us closer to our objective.

The second reason for writing only enough code to make the current failure message go away is that it lowers the mental burden in each step of the feedback loop process. It might seem like a trivial distinction to only write enough code to make the current failure message go away as opposed to writing enough code to make the test pass, but often the difference between the two is quite substantial.

Repeat steps 3 and 4 until the test passes

Unless the first line of code written happens to make the test pass, it will be necessary to keep adding bits of code, checking the result of the test after each change.

Repeat from step 1 with a new objective

Once the test passes, you're done, and you can begin the process again with a new specification.

We saw earlier that none of this feedback loop process necessarily has to have anything to do with automated testing. The feedback loop style of programming can be quite effective all by itself, even when the tests are performed manually. But when we combine feedback loops with automated testing, the process becomes all the more powerful. Let's take a look at what that means.

3.3.2   Automating the feedback loop

Despite the fact that we're going to replace manual tests with automated ones, the steps in the feedback loop stay exactly the same. Let's take another look at the feedback loop steps, this time using automated tests instead of manual ones.

Specify an objective

We'll use an example related to the expression parser from Chapter 1. Here are the specifications related to parsing an expression with an explicit multiplication operator.

1. **Scenario**: when the expression involves multiplication with an explicit operator (example: 2*x)

    a. **Expectation**: the root of the expression is the multiplication operator. If for example the expression is 2*x, the parsed expression's root is *.

    b. **Expectation**: the left child is the first operand. If for example the expression is 2*x, the parsed expression's first child is 2.

    c. **Expectation**: the right child is the second operand. If for example the expression is 2*x, the parsed expression's second child is x.

The first thing we'll do is write a test.

Devise a test that can be performed to see if #1 is done

The test code below should look familiar to you based on the tests we saw in Chapter 1. In this test we're asserting that when the expression involves multiplication with an explicit operator, the expression's root is *.

```
RSpec.describe "expression parser" do
  context "the expression involves multiplication with an" \
          "explicit operator" do
    it "assigns the multiplication operator to the root" do
```

```
      expression = Expression.parse("2*x")
      expect(expression.root).to eq("*")
    end
  end
end
```

Now we can run the test and see what kind of failure we get.

Perform the test devised in step 2

The test failure tells us that it doesn't recognize the class name `Expression`, which makes sense because we haven't yet defined such a class.

```
Failures:

  1) expression parser the expression involves multiplication
       with an explicit operator assigns the multiplication
       operator to the root
     Failure/Error: expression = Expression.parse("2*x")

     NameError:
       uninitialized constant Expression

           expression = Expression.parse("2*x")
                        ^^^^^^^^^^
     # ./expression_parser_spec.rb:4:in 'block (3 levels)
       in <top (required)>'

Finished in 0.02398 seconds (files took 0.06847 seconds to load)
1 example, 1 failure
```

Let's now write just enough code to make the failure message go away.

Do some work toward the objective (write a line of code)

Remember that we're not trying to write enough code to make the test pass, only enough to make the current test failure go away. This way we lighten the mental burden and avoid coding speculatively.

```
class Expression
end

RSpec.describe "expression parser" do
  context "the expression involves multiplication with an" \
        "explicit operator" do
    it "assigns the multiplication operator to the root" do
      expression = Expression.parse("2*x")
```

```
      expect(expression.root).to eq("*")
    end
  end
end
```

Now we can run the test again and see what new failure message we get.

Repeat steps 3 and 4 until the test passes

This time the failure is an error that says there is no method called parse, which is true.

```
Failures:

  1) expression parser the expression involves multiplication
       with an explicit operator assigns the multiplication
       operator to the root
     Failure/Error: expression = Expression.parse("2*x")

     NoMethodError:
       undefined method 'parse' for Expression:Class

           expression = Expression.parse("2*x")
                                   ^^^^^^^
     # ./expression_parser_spec.rb:7:in 'block (3 levels)
       in <top (required)>'

Finished in 0.00281 seconds (files took 0.06848 seconds to load)
1 example, 1 failure
```

We can address this failure by defining a parse method on the Expression class.

```
class Expression
  def self.parse
  end
end
```

Running the test again, we get an error that says parse was given 1 argument when it expected 0. This is because our test is calling Expression.parse("2*x") but we haven't defined parse to take any arguments.

```
Failures:

  1) expression parser the expression involves multiplication with an
       explicit operator assigns the multiplication operator to the root
     Failure/Error:
```

```
        def self.parse
        end

    ArgumentError:
      wrong number of arguments (given 1, expected 0)
    # ./expression_parser_spec.rb:2:in 'parse'
    # ./expression_parser_spec.rb:9:in 'block (3 levels)
        in <top (required)>'
```

```
Finished in 0.00286 seconds (files took 0.06984 seconds to load)
1 example, 1 failure
```

We can make this failure go away by redefining `parse` to take an argument. We don't actually need to do anything with the argument yet so let's not, since that would be speculative coding.

```
class Expression
  def self.parse(value)
  end
end
```

Now, when we try to call `expression.root` in the test, we get an error that says `undefined method 'root' for nil:NilClass`. This means that `expression` is nil. Why is `expression` nil? Because in the test we're assigning `expression` to the return value of `Expression.parse`, but `Expression.parse` doesn't return anything.

```
Failures:

  1) expression parser the expression involves multiplication
      with an explicit operator assigns the multiplication
      operator to the root
    Failure/Error: expect(expression.root).to eq("*")

    NoMethodError:
      undefined method 'root' for nil:NilClass

          expect(expression.root).to eq("*")
                            ^^^^^
    # ./expression_parser_spec.rb:14:in 'block (3 levels)
      in <top (required)>'
```

```
Finished in 0.00271 seconds (files took 0.07079 seconds to load)
1 example, 1 failure
```

We can fix this problem by making `Expression` return an instance of itself.

```
class Expression
  def self.parse(value)
    new
  end
end
```

Now we get a slightly different error: instead of complaining that there's no method `root` for `NilClass`, the error says there's no method `root` for `Expression`.

```
Failures:

  1) expression parser the expression involves multiplication
       with an explicit operator assigns the multiplication
       operator to the root
     Failure/Error: expect(expression.root).to eq("*")

     NoMethodError:
       undefined method 'root' for #<Expression:0x00000001012d0fd0>

             expect(expression.root).to eq("*")
                                ^^^^^
     # ./expression_parser_spec.rb:11:in 'block (3 levels)
         in <top (required)>'

Finished in 0.00332 seconds (files took 0.07894 seconds to load)
1 example, 1 failure
```

We can fix this by adding a `root` method.

```
class Expression
  def self.parse(value)
    new
  end

  def root
  end
end
```

Now, finally, we get a more meaningful error. We expected `expression.root` to be `*`, but it was `nil`.

```
Failures:

  1) expression parser the expression involves multiplication
       with an explicit operator assigns the multiplication
       operator to the root
     Failure/Error: expect(expression.root).to eq("*")
```

```
    expected: "*"
         got: nil

    (compared using ==)
 # ./expression_parser_spec.rb:14:in 'block (3 levels)x
    in <top (required)>'
```

```
Finished in 0.01143 seconds (files took 0.06977 seconds to load)
1 example, 1 failure
```

How should we make this failure go away? By adding the simplest code that we possibly can.

```
class Expression
  def self.parse(value)
    new
  end

  def root
    "*"
  end
end
```

Now the test passes.

```
Finished in 0.00259 seconds (files took 0.0609 seconds to load)
1 example, 0 failures
```

Why did we choose to use such a lazy solution?

The answer is because we want to avoid two certain evils. The first is that we want to avoid owning code that's neither covered by a test nor has a good reason not to be covered by a test. When a system has behaviors that users need but which aren't covered by tests, then changes to the system can cause silent bugs, bugs which escape detection by automated tests and which make it to production without our knowledge.

The second reason is because, again, we want to avoid coding *speculatively*. We want our system to contain just enough code to meet the system's requirements and no more. If we add code beyond the bare minimum that our tests force us to add, then we risk owning superfluous code, code which adds cost for no benefit.

3.4 TDD for system specs

TDD can be harder with system specs than with lower-level specs since the details of what the test will be doing are often less clear. In order to write the entire system spec first, you would almost have to imagine the fully-finished feature, with all its UI details, before you could write the test. I don't think that's really a reasonable thing to ask of oneself. Does that mean we can't do TDD for system specs?

No, we can still do TDD, or at least some version of it. The key is just to be a little more vague. Even if we can't imagine e.g. the specific DOM elements our test is going to need to interact with, we can still imagine what the test will be at a high level. Here, for example, are the steps for a test for deleting a customer.

1. Create a customer

2. Sign in

3. Visit the customer index page

4. Click on "Delete" on the customer row

5. Expect that the customer is no longer present on the page

By starting with a very high-level, non-technical test, we can separate the "what" from the "how". How exactly are we going to locate the right "Delete" button in the customer list, even though there might be multiple identical "Delete" buttons? Who cares. We don't need to concern ourselves with that detail yet.

Once we've come up with the high-level specification, we can take the easiest next step, which is to simply paste the specification into the test as a series of comments.

```
RSpec.describe "deleting a customer", type: :system do
  it "removes the customer from the page" do
    # Create a customer
    # Sign in
    # Visit the customer index page
    # Click on "Delete" on the customer row
    # Expect that the customer is no longer present on the page
  end
end
```

Once I've sketched out my test in the form of comments, I convert the comments to working code by using the following feedback loop:

For each comment...

1. Replace the comment with the code that I think will make that step work (e.g. replace "Create a customer" with `customer = create(:customer)`)

2. Run the test to see if my change behaves as expected

3. If not, make a correction and repeat step 2

4. Optional: if it's impossible for this line of the test to execute successfully due to missing application code, write the application code needed in order for this line to execute. I make this judgment on a case-by-case basis.

5. Move to next line and start again from step 1

Here's what the above test might look like after a few iterations of this loop.

```
RSpec.describe "deleting a customer", type: :system do
  it "removes the customer from the page" do
    customer = create(:customer)
    user = create(:user)
    login_as(user, scope: :user)
    # Visit the customer index page
    # Click on "Delete" on the customer row
    # Expect that the customer is no longer present on the page
  end
end
```

Again, I personally find it unrealistic to try to write an entire system spec before writing any of the application code. So I don't try. Instead, I build my system spec layer by layer until it behaves the way I want it to.

3.5 Common objections to TDD

Sometimes it's hard to sell test-driven development to your boss or co-workers. Sometimes it's hard to sell TDD to yourself. Here are some of the common objections to TDD along with their refutations.

3.5.1 Is TDD worth the extra time it takes?

Many developers and managers believe that TDD takes *extra* time. It's true that TDD takes extra time when you're first learning it. But once you get past a certain level of fluency, it's not a time-adder but a great time-saver.

It's also commonly believed that TDD saves time in the long run although it costs extra time in the short term. My experience is that this is emphatically un-true. When I try to code something without tests, I often find myself regretting my lack of tests within *minutes*. Remember, the alternative to automated testing is not no testing but manual testing. And due to natural human fallibility and laziness, the manual testing that developers perform (most certainly including myself) tends to be ad-hoc, incomplete and too infrequent. By the time manual testing reveals problems, the problems are too deep to be easily fixable. Provided the developer is already sufficiently comfortable with the process, the investment of test-driven development tends to pay off not within weeks or months but within minutes.

3.5.2   I don't know if I have the discipline to practice TDD all the time.

As we saw earlier in this chapter, TDD doesn't actually require much discipline. I think the alternative, manual testing, actually requires a lot more discipline. The hard part about practicing TDD isn't to muster up the discipline, it's to push through the difficult learning phase before TDD feels easy and natural. But luckily, that's a one-time expense.

3.5.3   How can I practice TDD if I'm not given clear requirements?

This one has an easy answer. You can't! But in that case, you can't code using any other methodology either. There's no way around the fact that you have to decide what to do before you can do it.

Sometimes the only way to nail down the requirements of a change is to do a *spike*: a quick, experimental, possibly sloppy and test-free exploration. It's usually much easier to look at a crappy idea and imagine how it could be better than it is to try to come up with a good idea out of thin air.

Spikes aren't incompatible with TDD. Don't make the mistake of thinking the only purpose of code is to create a work product. Code isn't only a medium for building; it's also a medium for thinking. If you're not sure yet what you want to build, you can mess around with some scratch code for a bit until it becomes clear to you. Then you can blow away the scratch code and start anew using TDD.

Lastly, I hope you don't practice TDD because you feel like it's the "right" way to code or the way you're "supposed" to code. If you do choose to practice TDD, I hope you do so because you believe it's an *advantageous* way to code, with your motivation being not guilt but rational reasoning.

Chapter 4

Writing meaningful tests

Having tests is obviously better than not having tests, but not all ways of writing tests are equally good. Tests are more valuable when they're *meaningful*. What does it mean for a test to be meaningful?

A test is meaningful to the degree that it forces the system under test to conform to the system's behavior specifications. A test is meaningful if it tests not just means to ends, but ends themselves.

It's hard to overstate the importance of this principle. Most of the test suites I've seen in my career have, sadly, had an acute lack of meaningful tests. Instead of targeting ends, they target means. As a result, the tests do little to help give a high-level understanding of what the system is supposed to do. Writing tests that target means results in tests that are tightly coupled to the system's incidental implementation details. This means that instead of enabling liberal refactoring— what is supposed to be one of the primary benefits of well-written tests—the tests actually make design changes harder.

I have a strong suspicion that many of the developers who have tried testing and either don't get it or don't like it have mainly experienced a non-meaningful style of testing. Sadly, many educational resources and engineering leaders teach a non-meaningful style of testing, and many production test suites provide examples that are of dubious meaningfulness. This is another negative effect of non-meaningful tests: they give testing a bad name, and dampen the enthusiasm of developers who are trying to learn testing.

So, how do we write tests that are meaningful?

4.1   The difference between ends and means

When we're testing something, we can focus either on means or ends. If we're testing a stapler, for example, we could test the means by examining the stapler and asserting that it has all the right parts to be able to staple three sheets of paper together, or we could just actually use the stapler to staple three sheets of paper

together and assert that the papers are bound together. Here are a few examples of
ends assertions versus means assertions.

Ends assertion	Means assertion
The stapler can staple three sheets of paper together	The stapler has all the right parts
The stapler can staple 20 sheets of paper together	The stapler has space to fit 20 sheets of paper and staples that are big enough for 20 sheets of paper
The stapler can staple sheets of paper together repeatedly	The stapler has a hinge and a spring

A test that checks for the presence of a spring in a stapler, for example, is neither
necessary nor helpful. Such a test doesn't provide any additional assurance beyond
what the behavior tests provide. If the stapler's spring were to be removed, then
the test that asserts that the stapler can be used multiple times would fail, rendering
the spring-presence test redundant. Having a test that only tests implementation is
actually worse than having no test at all, since it provides no value but gives a false
sense of accomplishment.

4.2   How the ends and means principle applies to Rails tests

Here are a couple tests that target means rather than ends. The first test asserts that
the User model has a `has_many :posts` association. The second asserts that the
Post model `belongs_to :user`.

```
RSpec.describe User, type: :model do
  it { should have_many(:posts) }
end

RSpec.describe Post, type: :model do
  it { should belong_to(:user) }
end
```

These tests are equivalent to checking for a spring in a stapler. If the relationship between users and posts were to be severed, the tests above would fail, but so
would any tests that target the behavior that these associations enable.

Here's another example of tests that target means rather than ends.

```
it { is_expected.to have_many(:comments).dependent(:nullify) }
it { is_expected.to have_many(:feed_events).dependent(:delete_all) }
```

```
it { is_expected.to have_many(:mentions).dependent(:delete_all) }
it { is_expected.to have_many(:notifications).dependent(:delete_all) }
it { is_expected.to have_many(:page_views).dependent(:delete_all) }
```

Instead of asserting for the mere presence of associations, it would be more meaningful to make assertions on the behaviors that these associations enable. Why do dependent comments get nullified while dependent feed events get deleted? It would be helpful if there were tests that demonstrated the scenarios where this behavior is relevant and made assertions that would fail if the proper assertions weren't present.

Here's another test that targets means rather than ends, this time in a less obvious way.

```
RSpec.describe AccountDomainBlock do
  let(:account) { Fabricate(:account) }

  it 'removes blocking cache after creation' do
    Rails.cache.write(
      "exclude_domains_for:#{account.id}",
      'a.domain.already.blocked'
    )

    expect {
      block_domain_for_account('a.domain.blocked.later')
    }.to change {
      Rails.cache.exist?("exclude_domains_for:#{account.id}")
    }.to(false)
  end

  it 'removes blocking cache after destruction' do
    block = block_domain_for_account('domain')
    Rails.cache.write("exclude_domains_for:#{account.id}", 'domain')

    expect {
      block.destroy!
    }.to change {
      Rails.cache.exist?("exclude_domains_for:#{account.id}")
    }.to(false)
  end

  private

  def block_domain_for_account(domain)
    Fabricate(
      :account_domain_block,
      account: account,
      domain: domain
```

```
    )
  end
end
```

This test deals directly with values in the Rails cache. But caching is never an end in itself, only a means to performance improvements. I personally almost never write tests that are aware of caching. If I want to make an assertion that forces my code to bust a cache, I check the place where the value comes *out* of the cache, the place where the value actually matters. The test doesn't know anything about the caching but the test will fail if the cache busting fails. This way not only is my test more meaningful because it targets ends instead of means, but my test is also less tightly coupled from my implementation, allowing me to change my implementation without having to change the tests.

4.3   Nested ends and means

What exactly decides what's an end and what's a means?

Machines often contain other machines inside them. For example, a stapler contains a spring. A spring is quite a simple machine. It doesn't have a lot of specifications to meet. It can't be subdivided into smaller parts.

When you break a machine down into smaller and smaller parts, eventually you reach the "bottom" where the parts can no longer be divided. With a stapler, the bottom is reached quite quickly, since a stapler is so simple. Other machines of course are more complicated, for instance airplanes.

The most important property of an airplane is that it can fly. In a sense that's the only thing about an airplane that matters. But it would obviously be dumb if "can it fly?" were the only test that were ever performed on an airplane design. Working in that way would result in long, expensive feedback loops. We'd crash the airplane thousands of times before we got it working.

The airplane's design can be developed and tested more efficiently if we test certain parts independently. The airplane's engines, for example, can be tested even without attaching the engines to an airplane.

The engines in an airplane are, in a sense, analogous to the spring in a stapler. But in another important sense they're much different. A spring is a single part with virtually no interesting behavior to test. An engine is a complicated machine which itself has many parts. A stapler's spring is useless outside the stapler. It's only a means to an end and nothing else. An engine is a means to an end, but it's also an end in itself with its own supporting means. So when deciding what's a means and what's an end, it's important to realize that not everything is just one or the other. Some things are both.

4.4 How to decide what kinds of tests to write

Remember that in testing, there's no such thing as correct or incorrect. There are only costs and benefits. Different types of tests have different costs and benefits. Let's take a look at what our options are, how they compare to one another, and how to decide among them.

4.4.1 System tests and unit tests, a cost/benefit analysis

Of the many types of Rails tests one could write, let's set them all aside for a moment and consider just two types of tests: system tests and unit tests. System tests are tests that exercise the entire stack, from the web server to the database to the HTML, CSS and JavaScript. Unit tests don't have one single agreed-upon definition, but for our purposes we can define a unit test as a test that exercises a small piece of code in isolation. That is, no web server, no database, no HTML or CSS, just [insert language here] code, in our case Ruby.

The costs and benefits of system tests

What are the relative costs and benefits of system tests and unit tests as we've defined them here? System tests tend to be expensive to run and expensive to write. They're expensive to run because it takes time to start a web server, generate test data in the database, wait for page loads and so on. System tests are expensive to write because they have the most dependencies a test could possibly have, and it takes time and effort to determine what all the dependencies are for a particular test and how to satisfy them. Adding to the expense of writing system tests is the fact that it's often non-trivial to figure out how to write test code that manipulates the browser to do what the test needs to do. Furthermore, the nature of system tests makes them susceptible to flakiness (a condition where a test occasionally fails at random even though nothing has changed—see chapter 16) which can be quite expensive to diagnose and fix.

With all these downsides, why bother with system tests?

System tests are the only type of test that proves that all the parts of your system are successfully working together. Without system tests, we could theoretically have a web application with a fully passing suite of unit tests, even if the application is unable to successfully serve a single request. So even though system tests are expensive, they serve an indispensable role that's worth their high price.

The costs and benefits of unit tests

Unit tests have the exact opposite costs and benefits as system tests. Relative to system tests, unit tests are cheap to run and cheap to write. System tests often take several seconds to run whereas the execution time for unit tests is usually almost negligible. The trade-off is that unit tests tell you nothing about whether the individual components and layers of a system are successfully working together.

Dwelling for a moment longer in this simplified world where our only options are system tests and unit tests, what, given the trade-offs we've just seen, would be a rational testing strategy?

Most behaviors in an application have a "happy path", one or two obvious error/failure scenarios, and some number of edge cases. With this in mind, developing a testing strategy is an optimization problem: we want to achieve satisfactory test coverage while incurring the smallest cost possible.

Cost/benefit optimization

What if we were to do all system tests and no unit tests, or vice versa? The problem with doing all system tests would be that our test suite would be very wasteful. Most of our tests would spend a lot of time simply creating the background environment needed to exercise the behavior we're interested in, which for most of our tests would be almost identical. (We could create the background environment once and then perform multiple tests once we have it, but that would cause our tests not to be isolated, potentially leading to flakiness and other problems, and plus it would make our tests hard to understand.)

If we used all unit tests and no system tests, our test suite would be wonderfully fast but it would be of very limited value. There would be nothing to show us that our system works as a whole.

What if we used a minimal number of system tests—perhaps one for the happy path and one or two more for failure cases—and then used fast unit tests for all the edge cases? This way we'd get a reasonable level of confidence that our system works as a whole, but without the wasteful redundancy that we'd get by using system tests for everything. This approach does take a calculated risk, since we are foregoing the level of guarantee that we'd get by having system tests for absolutely everything, but having system tests for everything would be unaffordably expensive. The same way we don't wear crash helmets and flame-retardant every time we drive to the corner store, there's a certain level of testing beyond which more investment doesn't justify the payoff.

Now that we've considered the trade-offs between system tests and unit tests, let's bring some more of the complexity of the real world into the picture and look at all the different types of Rails tests.

4.4.2   System specs

As we've seen, system tests (or system *specs* in RSpec terminology) are tests that exercise the full application stack. System specs provide the indispensible benefit of demonstrating that all layers of the application work together as specified, but they tend to be expensive to write and expensive to run. In light of this trade-off,

I like to write a "smoke test" (as in, when you turn on the device, does it emit smoke?) for the happy path and a couple of non-happy path scenarios. This way I get some evidence that the whole stack works together without spending a huge amount on expensive system specs.

4.4.3 Model specs

Before we can meaningfully talk about model specs, it will help to get some clarity on what exactly a model is. Speaking most broadly, model is a simplified version of some concept in order to make that concept more suitable to work with. For example, a road atlas is a model of a road system. In the model, most of the real characteristics of the land on which the roads lie are left out. The user of the atlas doesn't want a satellite photo of the terrain, they want a useful representation of the part of the terrain they care about, the roads.

An application model is the same. It's a simplified version of some concept in order to make that concept more suitable to work with. In Rails, it just so happens that models are often backed by database tables. This is an implementation of the *Active Record* design pattern, an idea that predates Rails. A model *can* use the Active Record pattern and inherit from `ActiveRecord::Base` but it doesn't have to. Note that Rails' model folder is called `app/models`, not `app/active_record_models`.

I personally think it makes sense for most of a software system's behavior to be expressed in the form of a model. Recall from Chapter 2 that I didn't put the expression parser code into a class called `ExpressionParser` or (God forbid) `ExpressionParserService`. I conceived of a *model* called `Expression` which can model the aspects of an expression that the program cares about. The same way a road atlas is not a satellite photo, the `Expression` object probably won't model every conceivable detail of a mathematical expression, just the ones that make it easier to do the work we need to do.

In my Rails apps, the majority of the code is in the models, most of which are Plain Old Ruby Objects (POROs) which don't inherit from Active Record. Therefore, most of the tests in my test suites are model specs.

4.4.4 Request specs

As we've seen, system specs exercise the entire application stack. Request specs exercise *almost* the entire stack. Instead of manipulating your application via the browser and making assertions about what's on the page, request specs manipulate your application by sending HTTP requests to it and then making assertions about the responses.

Looking at testing again through the lens of costs and benefits, request specs give a little less end-to-end assurance than system specs, but they're also less expensive to write and run. I often find myself needing to test some piece of behavior (for example, a redirect fork) which doesn't depend at all on the DOM. To bring the browser into the picture would simply add wasteful overhead. In these cases I drop down to the request level so that I can cover the behavior I want to and achieve it more economically than I could with system specs.

4.4.5 Job specs

Background jobs exist so that we may run certain parts of our Rails code asynchronously in the background. Unlike models, which exist to express the system's behavior in an understandable way, background jobs exist purely for performance reasons.

Looking at the job below, what kind of tests might we write to ensure the job is working as specified?

```
class UpdateShipmentCacheJob < ApplicationJob
  queue_as :default

  def perform(shipment_id)
    Shipment.find(shipment_id).update_cache!
  end
end
```

Actually, I don't think there's any kind of test we could write for this job that would bring much benefit. We could write a test that asserts, say, that `update_cache!` gets called, and that would have more than zero value, but only slightly more than zero. The value of such a test is so small that I personally wouldn't even bother writing it.

What about tests that assert that certain jobs get enqueued? Again, this sort of test has more than zero value, but only slightly more than zero. Instead of doing this, I usually prefer to configure background jobs to run inline (as opposed to running asynchronously or getting skipped) and then assert for the result that the background job produces. To put it another way, I test for the behavior I'm interested in and treat the fact that the behavior is achieved via a background job as an incidental detail.

Job specs seem to be an area where it's particularly easy to get verification mixed up with specification. There are two questions that could be asked about a job: 1) did the behavior *happen*? and 2) does the behavior match its *specifications*? For the question of whether the behavior of the job happened, I'm not sure that tests are usually the most fitting device to use. I think production monitoring probably makes more sense in most cases.

For the question of whether the behavior matches its specifications, the fact that the behavior happens to live inside of a job is only an incidental detail. In fact, I don't think it's appropriate for much behavior to live inside a job. Again, background jobs don't exist to aid with code design, they exist in order to execute code in the background. Except for trivial cases, I think it's better to move the behavior that jobs execute out of the job and into a model.

4.4.6 Mailer specs

Like jobs, mailers don't exist to model application behavior. Mailers exist to, of course, send mail. Just like with jobs, any non-trivial behavior in a mailer can be moved to a model and tested there.

4.4.7 Helper specs

A helper in Rails is a method that abstracts away a small bit of view-related behavior. Helpers provide a good example of why a programmer's testing abilities rarely exceed design abilities. It's very easy for helpers to become "junk drawers". If each helper file is a convoluted mess, then the tests will by necessity be a convoluted mess too.

Luckily, the question of when to use helper specs is clear: for each helper you have in your application, you can have one helper spec. Just don't let the helpers turn into a junk drawer.

4.4.8 View specs

Why do we have separate concepts of view and controller? Why not put all the view and controller code together in one file? The answer of course is that that would make the code too hard to understand. A view file is easiest to understand if it only contains markup and behavior that's directly related to presentation.

View-related code tends not to contain a lot of behavior. It's usually mostly static. Furthermore, view code is usually a means to an end rather than an end in itself. To me, it's much more meaningful to use system specs to test the higher-level behavior that view code enables rather than to test the view code itself directly.

4.4.9 ViewComponent specs

View-related code is usually trivially simple but not always. Sometimes, for example, there's a form component whose state depends on a lot of different inputs. Complex view-related logic like this often causes the code in the view to become messy and convoluted. In an effort to tidy up some of the view code, sometimes the complex logic is moved to a helper, but this doesn't usually fix much, it only relocates the mess.

Why shouldn't view-related logic be object-oriented? Why shouldn't it have encapsulation and abstraction? Why shouldn't it be easy to test in isolation without having to involve irrelevant dependencies?

These to me are the problems that are solved by ViewComponent[1], a library created by Joel Hawksley at GitHub. ViewComponent allows pieces of views to be modeled as objects with encapsulated data and behavior. There's nothing particularly sacred about ViewComponent, and there's no reason other libraries couldn't implement similar ideas. I personally use ViewComponent because I know of no other similar library (and because Joel happens to be a friend of mine!).

Even though ViewComponent is a third-party library that doesn't come with Rails, the ideas that ViewComponent bring to the table are so important to me that I couldn't omit ViewComponent from this book. To repeat what I'm said a number of times elsewhere in this book, testing and application code design are deeply interdependent. It's not possible to become an excellent tester without also being an excellent designer. I don't think it's possible to adequately test complex view-related logic without breaking it up into physically and conceptually independent pieces which can each be conveniently tested without their dependencies.

4.5   When to write a test and when not to

As we've seen, there are certain categories of tests that I think should be skipped entirely. That's not to say that I think it makes sense to leave any parts of a system entirely untested. But are there exceptions? Are there any cases where it makes sense *not* to write a test?

Remember that testing isn't about right and wrong but about costs and benefits. Rare though they are, there are cases where the cost of writing a test does outweigh the benefit. On the rare occasions that my instincts tell me I might be dealing with such a case, I ask myself the following five questions.

1. Is the behavior likely to ever break?

2. If the behavior were to fail, would it fail silently?

3. If the behavior were to fail, would it fail frequently?

4. If the behavior were to fail, would the consequences be severe?

5. Is the test easy to write?

If any one of the answers to these questions is a yes, I write the test. If and only if *all* of the answers are negative do I skip the test.

I might skip, for example, a test for downloading an internal employee holiday calendar. The feature is unlikely to break. If it were to fail, it wouldn't fail silently. The consequences would be extremely low. The test might be really annoying to write. In this case it would probably be more economical to just skip the test and let someone complain if the feature breaks.

---

[1] https://viewcomponent.org/

4.6 The aggregate benefit of tests

Even though I sometimes skip tests in very specific rare cases, that's much different from a policy of writing test only for features that are "important". It's common to want to get some sort of 80/20 benefit by only covering the most important 20% of the codebase with tests. I think this way of thinking focuses on the benefit of individual tests while missing the *aggregate* benefit of tests.

Either your level of test coverage gives you sufficient confidence to refactor *anything and everything* or it doesn't. If, before refactoring, I have to stop and wonder whether this area is tested well enough to allow for refactoring, then my test suite is woefully underserving me. The difference between the design quality of a codebase that has undergone regular liberal refactorings and one that has only gotten occasional local refactorings is absolutely night and day. If you treat tests as only being good for catching bugs then you miss this ability. And ironically, if you can't liberally refactor, you'll probably have more bugs too.

4.7 Coupling and refactoring

Some developers hold a policy of favoring system specs over model specs out of a belief that model specs create too tight of coupling between tests and application code and therefore hinder refactoring. As we've seen, tests can either target ends or target means. Tests that target means tend to be much more tightly coupled to implementation details than tests that target ends. Model specs can be written in such a way as to be very tightly coupled to the implementation, or they can leave plenty of room for refactoring. Rarely should one have to resort to the extra expenses of system specs just for the sake of loose coupling. As long as they focus on ends rather than means, model specs are usually loosely coupled enough.

4.8 In a model, do I need to test every method?

Should every method in a model have a corresponding test?

The aim of testing isn't to cover every method but to cover every *behavior*. Sometimes this means a one-to-one mapping between model methods and tests and sometimes it doesn't.

4.9 Testing private methods

Private methods exist for two purposes. The first is reduce the surface area of an object's public API. The smaller and simpler an object is from the perspective of an outside client, the easier the object will be to understand. The other purpose of private methods is to indicate what's safe to refactor. Any method that's private will not be used by any outside client[2], and so can be renamed, have its behavior changed, or be deleted altogether, all without risk of breaking any clients' behavior, provided the public API of the object still behaves the same.

The behavior in private methods can be addressed in one of three ways:

1. Skip testing the private methods' behavior

2. Test the private methods' behavior directly by using `Object#send` to bypass the methods' privateness

3. Test the private methods' behavior indirectly, though the object's public API

The first option, skipping the testing, is of course not a real solution. Testing the private methods using `Object#send` will of course physically work, but it will tightly couple the implementation of the object to its test, making the test brittle and the object hard to refactor. The last option, testing the private methods directly through the object's public API, is the way to go. This allows us to still test all the behavior we want to test while keeping the test loosely coupled from the code in the object under test. This way the test is robust and the code is easy to refactor.

4.10   The two-way influence of test design and code design

How do you write tests for an application? That depends a lot on how you structure the application. If you put most of your code in controllers, for example, then you naturally won't have as many model specs, since less of your code will live in models.

If you have huge model files, then you'll have huge model specs. If your UI is complicated and quirky, your system specs will probably be complicated and quirky too. If your domain model is tidy and easy to understand, then your tests can be tidy and easy to understand as well. If your domain model is muddy and nonsensical, then your tests will be muddy and nonsensical too.

A programmer's testing skills and design skills will move more or less in lock-step. When an application's code is a convoluted mess, it's virtually impossible to put clean and tidy tests on it. It's like trying to put a saddle and harness on a great white shark. It just doesn't work. It's also impossible to maintain clean code without the refactoring abilities provided by good tests.

As you work to build your testing skills, give equal attention to building your design skills as well. You can't improve one too much without the other.

---

[2]Provided, of course, that no client is using `Object#send` to naughtily bypass the private methods' privateness.

Chapter 5

Writing understandable tests

Tests are more than just a safety net to catch regressions. A test suite can serve as a guidebook to a system, showing what the system's parts are, how the parts relate to each other, which ideas are more and less important, and of course, how the parts of the system are supposed to behave.

A test suite, which, remember, is a structured collection of *behavior specifications*, can also serve as the backbone for a system's design.

It's common to think of a system's code as its "essence" and the tests as something secondary. I invite you to think of it the other way around. A system's code shows what the system does, but the system's application code doesn't have the last word. The application code is answerable to its tests, which in turn are answerable to no one. Because an application's tests are its specifications, whatever the tests specify is, by definition, correct.

If all the application code for a system were to be deleted but the tests were to be kept, the application code could in principle be recreated based on the tests.

So far we've mostly focused on writing new tests and running them. But in a production application, in addition to being written and run, tests often need to be understood and modified.

Individual tests also of course exist as part of a test suite. In addition to having tests that are individually easy to understand, it's also helpful to organize your test suite in a way that's easy to understand and work with.

5.1   Abstraction

Abstraction is the art of hiding distracting details and emphasizing essential information.

Abstraction is of course a well-known concept in programming. However, abstraction is usually applied mainly to application code, and applied very much less to tests.

Test code is responsible for jobs that vary widely in their relevance to the high-level meaning of the test. Test data has to be created, dependencies have to be initialized, code has to be finagled into the right state, assertions have to be made, and so on. It can be easy for the meaning of the test to be obscured by the incidental details of the test code.

Let's look at an example of how this can happen. Below is a description of a test for replying to a comment on an article. For the moment, don't think about *how* the code for this test might be written, just think about *what* is happening in the test.

- **Setup**

  1. Create an article in the database
  2. Create a comment for that article (so we have something to reply to)

- **Exercise**

  1. Visit the article
  2. Fill in the "reply" input with some text
  3. Click save

- **Assertion**

  1. Expect the page to show the reply that was just entered

Since it contains no code, the description above is all signal and no noise. Perhaps it might be nice if we could write all our tests like this but of course we have to convert the test into executable code, and naturally, some of the "gruntwork" code is going to add some noise to the test that will make it harder to understand. Below is a possible implementation of this test.[1]

```
RSpec.describe "Creating Comment", type: :feature, js: true do
  let(:user) { create(:user) }
  let(:raw_comment) { Faker::Lorem.paragraph }
  let(:article) do
    create(:article, user_id: user.id, show_comments: true)
  end

  before { sign_in user }

  it "User replies to a comment" do
    create(:comment, commentable_id: article.id, user_id: user.id)
    visit article.path.to_s
```

---

[1] This test was found in the public GitHub repository for Forem (https://github.com/forem/forem), an open source community platform.

```
find(".toggle-reply-form").click

find(
  :xpath,
  "//div[@class='actions']/form[@class='new_comment']/textarea"
).set(raw_comment)

find(
  :xpath,
  "//div[contains(@class, 'reply-actions')]/input[@name='commit']"
).click

expect(page).to have_text(raw_comment)
  end
end
```

Let's go through this test bit by bit, identifying the areas that could benefit from better abstraction. But first let's make sure we're clear on what this test is all about.

```
RSpec.describe "Creating Comment", type: :feature, js: true do
  it "User replies to a comment" do
  end
end
```

According to its top-level `describe` block, this test is about creating a comment. That's fine and good. The `it` block, though, reads a bit awkwardly. It reads as "it user replies to a comment". The "it" refers to the system under test. The `it` block should describe how "it" (the system) should behave. To me the way this test description is written is a sign that this test is not the result of a clearly-thought-out *specification*.

We saw in chapter 2 that we can develop specifications by thinking of various scenarios and the expected behavior in those scenarios. What might be the scenario and expectation for this particular test? One idea that comes to mind is "when a user submits a reply to a comment on an article (scenario), the body of the reply shows up on the article's page (expectation)". With that in mind, the test's shell might be revised as follows.

```
RSpec.describe "Creating Comment", type: :feature, js: true do
  context "user submits a reply to a comment on an article" do
    it "shows the reply on the article's page" do
    end
  end
end
```

Using this new shell, let's now look at the body of the test.

```
context "user submits a reply to a comment on an article" do
  it "shows the reply on the article's page" do
    create(:comment, commentable_id: article.id, user_id: user.id)
    visit article.path.to_s
    find(".toggle-reply-form").click

    find(
      :xpath,
      "//div[@class='actions']/form[@class='new_comment']/textarea"
    ).set(raw_comment)

    find(
      :xpath,
      "//div[contains(@class, 'reply-actions')]/input[@name='commit']"
    ).click

    expect(page).to have_text(raw_comment)
  end
end
```

One of the first things my attention is drawn to is raw_comment. What's so "raw" about it and why does it need to be raw?

The value is set to Faker::Lorem.paragraph (a paragraph's worth of random text, provided by the Faker library, but that doesn't shed any light on why this comment needs to be "raw".

```
let(:raw_comment) { Faker::Lorem.paragraph }
```

In addition to having a mysterious name, the very fact that raw_comment is not a hard-coded string hurts the understandability of the test. I hope you agree that the below version is slightly easier to understand.

```
context "user submits a reply to a comment on an article" do
  it "shows the reply on the article's page" do
    create(:comment, commentable_id: article.id, user_id: user.id)
    visit article.path.to_s
    find(".toggle-reply-form").click

    find(
      :xpath,
      "//div[@class='actions']/form[@class='new_comment']/textarea"
    ).set("This is a reply")

    find(
      :xpath,
      "//div[contains(@class, 'reply-actions')]/input[@name='commit']"
    ).click
```

```
      expect(page).to have_text("This is a reply")
    end
end
```

Now we can turn our attention to the noisiest part of the test, the `find` commands. One option for addressing this is to simply add a couple helper methods right in the same test file. In this case, near the bottom of the file, we've added two helper methods: `textarea` and `commit_button`.

```
RSpec.describe "Creating Comment", type: :feature, js: true do
  let(:user) { create(:user) }
  let(:article) do
    create(:article, user_id: user.id, show_comments: true)
  end

  before { sign_in user }

  context "user submits a reply to a comment on an article" do
    it "shows the reply on the article's page" do
      create(:comment, commentable_id: article.id, user_id: user.id)
      visit article.path.to_s
      find(".toggle-reply-form").click

      textarea.set("This is a reply")
      commit_button.click

      expect(page).to have_text("This is a reply")
    end
  end

  def textarea
    find(
      :xpath,
      "//div[@class='actions']/form[@class='new_comment']/textarea"
    )
  end

  def commit_button
    find(
      :xpath,
      "//div[contains(@class, 'reply-actions')]/input[@name='commit']"
    )
  end
end
```

Another way we can clean up this test is by using a *page object*. We'll take a look at page objects later in this chapter.

5.2   Helpful abstraction versus obfuscating indirection

Let's take another look at our "create a comment" test. Here it is the way I originally
found it.

```
RSpec.describe "Creating Comment", type: :feature, js: true do
  let(:user) { create(:user) }
  let(:raw_comment) { Faker::Lorem.paragraph }
  let(:article) do
    create(:article, user_id: user.id, show_comments: true)
  end

  before { sign_in user }

  it "User replies to a comment" do
    create(:comment, commentable_id: article.id, user_id: user.id)
    visit article.path.to_s
    find(".toggle-reply-form").click

    find(
      :xpath,
      "//div[@class='actions']/form[@class='new_comment']/textarea"
    ).set(raw_comment)

    find(
      :xpath,
      "//div[contains(@class, 'reply-actions')]/input[@name='commit']"
    ).click

    expect(page).to have_text(raw_comment)
  end
end
```

We could "clean up" the test by moving the noisy chunks of code into separate
methods and then calling those methods. In the example below the test has been
reduced to three tidy lines. What do you think?

```
RSpec.describe "Creating Comment", type: :feature, js: true do
  before { sign_in user }

  it "User replies to a comment" do
    create_setup_data
    submit_comment
    expect_correct_comment
  end

  def create_setup_data
    let(:user) { create(:user) }
```

```
    let(:raw_comment) { Faker::Lorem.paragraph }
    let(:article) do
      create(:article, user_id: user.id, show_comments: true)
    end
  end

  def submit_comment
    create(:comment, commentable_id: article.id, user_id: user.id)
    visit article.path.to_s
    find(".toggle-reply-form").click

    find(
      :xpath,
      "//div[@class='actions']/form[@class='new_comment']/textarea"
    ).set(raw_comment)

    find(
      :xpath,
      "//div[contains(@class, 'reply-actions')]/input[@name='commit']"
    ).click
  end

  def expect_correct_comment
    expect(page).to have_text(raw_comment)
  end
end
```

The test might superficially *look* cleaner but it's actually no easier to understand than before. In fact, it's harder to understand. The original version was messy but at least all its details were on full display and, with a little effort, we could work out the high-level meaning.

In the new version, the details are stolen away from us. What exactly might be happening inside of `create_setup_data`? There's nothing to go off of. It could be any data at all. The only way to get the slightest clue of what it's doing is to go look at its contents. And if an "abstraction" doesn't give you the slightest clue of what it's doing without looking at its contents, then it's a pretty poor abstraction indeed! Same story with `submit_comment` and `expect_correct_comment`.

Moral of the story: When a test is full of distracting details, simply moving the details behind methods isn't necessarily an improvement. Careful thought must be given to what abstractions the methods represent and why they're helpful.

5.3 Scoping

Many Rails test suites suffer from a "low resolution" problem. The contents of the `spec/models` folder, for example, might look something like this:

```
$ ls -1 spec/models
appointment_spec.rb
invoice_spec.rb
patient_spec.rb
user_spec.rb
```

The application may have a rich and complex hierarchy of behavior, but that behavior isn't reflected in the structure of the model tests. Instead, 100% of the application's model tests are shoehorned into a small number of test files whose names match the tables in the app's database. If you look inside of each test file, it's crammed with a hodgepodge of tests for dozens of different kinds of behaviors.

Why is the test code like this? Because it's a reflection of the application code, which is structured exactly the same way! Like the test files, the model files have a one-to-one relationship with the application's database tables.

```
$ ls -1 app/models
appointment.rb
invoice.rb
patient.rb
user.rb
```

If you look inside of each one of these model files, you'll find that the contents are just as much of a mixed bag as that of the test files. The `rails g scaffold appointment` command gave the developers two containers to put stuff in, one called `app/models/appointment.rb` and another called `spec/models/appointment_spec.rb`. Slowly over time, each one of these containers grew, a few lines of code at a time, into a monster.

How do we fix this? By slicing up the model code into smaller, more cohesive pieces.

I worked with Rails for years before I realized I could put things in `app/models` other than Active Record models. If for example the `Appointment` model had the concept of a recurrence rule, the recurrence rule logic could be moved into an object called `RecurrenceRule` which lives in `app/models/recurrence_rule.rb`. Or even better, the model could be put in a namespace and be called `Schedule::RecurrenceRule` and live at `app/models/schedule/recurrence_rule.rb`. The corresponding test could live in `spec/models/schedule/recurrence_rule_spec.rb`.

Important note: everything is connected to everything else. It's not possible to become excellent in testing without growing one's application architecture skills proportionally.

5.4 Specific versus general, concrete versus abstract

It's easier to see a specific example and then generalize from it than to see a general concept and then imagine the specific ways in which the concept might apply.

That's why our language is filled with vivid metaphors like "those who live in glass houses should not throw stones" instead of vague expressions like "you shouldn't criticize people for faults that you yourself possess". Metaphoric sayings are popular because they serve as specific, easy-to-picture examples of the more vague, more abstract concepts they convey. The general principle doesn't need to be directly stated because we can infer it from the specific example.

Code is also easier to understand when it's specific.

5.5 Cohesion

Every codebase is, in a sense, a story. Well-designed programs tell a coherent, easy-to-understand story. Other programs are poorly designed and tell a confusing, hard-to-understand story. And it's often the case that a program wasn't *designed* at all, and so no attempt was made to tell a coherent story. But there's some sort of story in the code no matter what.

If a codebase is like a story, a file in a codebase is perhaps like a chapter in a book. A well written-chapter will clearly let the reader know what the most important points are and will feature those important points most prominently. A chapter is most understandable when it principally sticks to just one topic.

The telling of the story will surely unavoidably require the conveyance of incidental details. When this happens, those incidental details are put in their proper place and not mixed confusingly with essential points. If a detail would pose too much of a distraction or an interruption, it gets moved to a footnote or appendix or parenthetical clause.

A piece of code is **cohesive** if a) everything in it shares one single idea and b) it doesn't mix incidental details with essential points.

Now let's talk about ways that cohesion tends to get lost as well as ways to maintain cohesion.

5.5.1 How cohesion gets lost

Fresh new projects are usually pretty easy to work with. This is because a) when you don't have very much code, it's easier to keep your code organized, and b) when the total amount of code is small, things have to be pretty disorganized in order for it to hurt.

Things get tougher as the project grows. Entropy (the tendency for all things to decline into disorder) unavoidably sets in. Unless there are constant efforts to fight back against entropy, the codebase grows increasingly disordered and hard to understand.

One common manifestation of entropy is the tendency for developers to hang new methods onto objects (or test cases onto test files) like ornaments on a Christmas tree. A developer is tasked with adding a new behavior. He or she goes looking for the object that seems like the most fitting home for that behavior. He or she adds the new behavior, which doesn't *perfectly* fit the object where it was placed, but the new code only makes the object, say, 5% less cohesive, and it's not clear where might be a better place for that behavior, so in it goes.

This ornament-hanging habit is allowed to take place because no individual "offense" appears to be all that bad. This is the nature of entropy: disorder sets in not because anything bad was done but simply because no one is going out of their way to stave off disorder.

Even though no individual change appears to be all that bad, the result of all these changes in aggregate is a surprisingly bad mess. The objects are huge. They confusingly mix unrelated ideas. Their essential points are obscured by incidental details. They're virtually impossible to understand. They lack cohesion.

How can this problem be prevented?

5.5.2   How cohesion can be preserved

The first key to maintaining cohesion in any particular piece of code is to make a clear distinction between what's **essential** and what's **incidental**.

Let's say I have, for example, a class called `Appointment`. The concerns of `Appointment` include, among other things, a start time, a client and some matters related to caching.

I would say that the start time and client are *essential* concerns of the appointment and that the caching is probably *incidental*. In the story of `Appointment`, start time and client are important highlights, whereas caching concerns are incidental details and should be tucked away in a footnote or appendix.

That explains how to identify incidental details *conceptually* but it doesn't explain how to separate incidental details *mechanically*. So, how do we do that?

The primary way I do this is to simply move the incidental details into different objects. Let's say for example that I have a `Customer` object with certain methods including one called `balance`.

Over time the balance calculation becomes increasingly complicated to the point that it causes `Customer` to lose cohesion. No problem: I can just move the guts of the `balance` method into a new object (a PORO) called `CustomerBalance` and delegate all the gory details of balance calculation to that object. Now `Customer` can once again focus on the essential points and forget about the incidental details.

Now, in this case it made perfect sense to recognize the concept of a customer balance as a brand new abstraction. But it doesn't always work out this way. In our earlier `Appointment` example, for example, it's maybe not so natural to take our caching concerns and conceive of them as a new extraction. It's not particularly clear how that would go.

What we can do in these cases, when we want to move an incidental detail out of an object but we can't put our finger on a befitting new abstraction, is we can use a mixin instead. I view mixins as a good way to hold a bit of code which has cohesion with itself but which doesn't quite qualify as an abstraction and so doesn't make sense as an object. For me, mixins usually don't have standalone value, and they're usually only ever "mixed in" to one object as opposed to being reusable.

(I could have said concern instead of mixin, but a) to me it's a distinction without a meaningful difference, and b) concerns come along with some conceptual baggage that I didn't want to bring into the picture here.)

So for our `Appointment` example, we could move the caching code into a mixin in order to get it out of `Appointment` so that `Appointment` could once again focus solely on its essential points and forget about its incidental details.

5.5.3   Where to put these newly-sprouted files

When I make an object more cohesive by breaking out its incidental details into new model file, you might wonder where I put that new file.

The short answer is that I put these files into `app/models`, with additional subfolders based on the meaning of the code.

So for the `Appointment`, I might have `app/models/appointment.rb` and `app/models/scheduling/appointment_caching.rb`, provided that the caching code is related specifically to scheduling. The rationale here is that the caching logic will only ever be relevant to scheduling whereas an appointment might be viewed in multiple contexts, e.g. sometimes scheduling and sometimes billing.

For the customer balance example, I might have `app/models/customer.rb` and `app/models/billing/customer_balance.rb`. Again, a customer balance is always a billing concern whereas a customer could be looked at through a billing lens or conceivably through some other sort of lens.

Note that even though `appointment_caching.rb` is a mixin or concern, I don't put it in a `concerns` or `mixins` folder. That's because I believe in organizing files by meaning rather than type. I find that doing so makes it easier to find what I want to find when I want to find it.

As mentioned earlier in this book, tests can be thought of as executable specifications, as the definitive source of truth for a system's desired behavior. If tests serve such an important role as this, then it would of course be good if they're easy to understand. What makes for an understandable test?

5.6   Shared examples

Sometimes two areas of an application share an identical piece of behavior. This can create some awkward choices for testing. We could simply duplicate the tests for the two areas of code but then we'd be burdened with having to keep the two areas synchronized. We could write tests for one of the two areas and use the correct functioning of the first area as evidence that the second area is also working, but that would leave a big gap in our test coverage since the second area would be missing tests. Another option is to use *shared examples*. Share examples are an RSpec feature that allows you to write a piece of test code once and reuse it in multiple places. Here's an example of shared examples from the RSpec documentation.

```
require "set"

RSpec.shared_examples "a collection object" do
  describe "<<" do
    it "adds objects to the end of the collection" do
      collection << 1
      collection << 2
      expect(collection.to_a).to match_array([1, 2])
    end
  end
end

RSpec.describe Array do
  it_behaves_like "a collection object" do
    let(:collection) { Array.new }
  end
end

RSpec.describe Set do
  it_behaves_like "a collection object" do
    let(:collection) { Set.new }
  end
end
```

At first glance, shared examples might seem like a nice way to keep tests tidy and DRY. Unfortunately, shared examples are actually fraught with problems.

5.6.1   Obfuscation

When part of a test is defined by a shared example, it means that some of its tests are hidden away somewhere else. The example above is self-contained in one snippet, making it easy to take in the shared example definition with its usages as a single group. In a production codebase the definition of a shared example is usually in a different file from the tests that use it.

A shared example is a function. It can be called, and data can be passed to it. But it's a very awkward sort of function. Instead of taking distinct arguments like most functions do, an it_behaves_like method accepts a block for an argument inside of which you can define any setup data that you want the shared example to have. But unlike normal functions which show all their parameters in their definitions, shared examples make use of values without giving any clues as to where they came from. Furthermore, a shared example will inherit the full scope of the test that includes it. This means the shared example will potentially become tightly coupled with the tests that include them. Values in the test can't be easily changed because who knows what's being used in a shared example.

Below is an example of a shared example that's used to test two similar classes, LoyaltyDiscount and SharedDiscount. If the shared example were stored in a different file than the tests for LoyaltyDiscount and SeasonalDiscount, it would be pretty hard to tell what the values for initial_amount, discount_rate and discount are.

```
# -------------------------------
# loyalty_discount_spec.rb

RSpec.describe LoyaltyDiscount do
  let(:initial_amount) { 100 }
  let(:discount_rate) { 0.20 }
  let(:discount) { LoyaltyDiscount.new }

  it_behaves_like "a discount applicator"
end

# -------------------------------
# seasonal_discount_spec.rb

RSpec.describe SeasonalDiscount do
  let(:initial_amount) { 100 }
  let(:discount_rate) { 0.10 }
  let(:discount) { SeasonalDiscount.new }

  it_behaves_like "a discount applicator"
end

# -------------------------------
# discount_applicator_shared_examples.rb

RSpec.shared_examples "a discount applicator" do
  it "correctly applies a percentage discount" do
    result = discount.apply_discount(
      initial_amount,
      discount_rate
    )

    expected = initial_amount * (1 - discount_rate)
    expect(result).to eq(expected)
  end
end
```

LoyaltyDiscount and SeasonalDiscount can be tested without resorting to shared examples. How? Simply repeat the tests.

```
RSpec.describe LoyaltyDiscount do
  let(:initial_amount) { 100 }
  let(:discount_rate) { 0.20 }
  let(:loyalty_discount) { LoyaltyDiscount.new }

  it "correctly applies a percentage discount" do
    result = loyalty_discount.apply_discount(
      initial_amount,
      discount_rate
    )

    expected = initial_amount * (1 - discount_rate)
    expect(result).to eq(expected)
  end
end

RSpec.describe SeasonalDiscount do
  let(:initial_amount) { 100 }
  let(:discount_rate) { 0.10 }
  let(:seasonal_discount) { SeasonalDiscount.new }

  it "correctly applies a percentage discount" do
    result = seasonal_discount.apply_discount(
      initial_amount,
      discount_rate
    )

    expected = initial_amount * (1 - discount_rate)
    expect(result).to eq(expected)
  end
end
```

In fact, we can improve these tests even further. What exactly does it mean to "correctly apply a percentage discount"? We can write a better description than that. The improvements below aren't related to shared examples, but the example test above might be misleading if it still contains all its original flaws.

```
RSpec.describe LoyaltyDiscount do
  let(:loyalty_discount) { LoyaltyDiscount.new }

  context "initial amount is $1.00 and discount rate is 20%" do
    let(:initial_amount) { 100 }
    let(:discount_rate) { 0.20 }

    it "sets the amount to $0.80" do
      new_amount = loyalty_discount.apply_discount(
        initial_amount,
        discount_rate
```

```
      )

      expect(new_amount).to eq(0.8)
    end
  end
end

RSpec.describe SeasonalDiscount do
  let(:seasonal_discount) { SeasonalDiscount.new }

  context "initial amount is $1.00 and discount rate is 20%" do
    let(:initial_amount) { 100 }
    let(:discount_rate) { 0.10 }

    it "sets the amount to $0.90" do
      new_amount = seasonal_discount.apply_discount(
        initial_amount,
        discount_rate
      )

      expect(new_amount).to eq(0.9)
    end
  end
end
```

We got away from shared examples by duplicating the test code that the shared example would have unified. But isn't duplication bad?

"Duplication" is short for "behavior duplication". Duplication is mainly bad when it poses a risk of two or more pieces of behavior getting out of sync due to a mistake, leaving one copy of the behavior correct and the other one incorrect. Since tests aren't behavior, they're not always susceptible to the same kinds of duplication mistakes as application code. See chapter 6 for details.

5.7 Using subject and let

RSpec's `subject` feature is an attempt to make tests more readable and less repetitive. Here's an example from the official RSpec documentation.[2]

```
RSpec.describe Array, "with some elements" do
  subject { [1, 2, 3] }

  it "has the prescribed elements" do
    expect(subject).to eq([1, 2, 3])
  end
end
```

_____

[2]https://rspec.info/features/3-12/rspec-core/subject/explicit-subject/

One of the problems with `subject` is that, rather than providing helpful abstraction, it creates harmful obfuscation. The word "subject" is always going to be less specific than whatever value a `subject` refers to.

Another problem with `subject` is that it can be hard to tell what value any particular `subject` is connected to. This problem is especially tricky in a large test which defines a `subject` and then overrides it one or more times.

I've never seen an instance of `subject` that wouldn't have been improved by just replacing `subject` with the thing it stands in for. I think `subject` is one of those RSpec features which simply shouldn't exist.

The `let` helper is a bit more nuanced. I use `let` in virtually all my tests, although it can certainly be used in ways that hurt rather than help.

Setup data in a test has to be assigned somehow. When a piece of setup data is created right inside an `it` block, its value can just be assigned to a local variable. When a value has to span multiple `it` blocks, that's no longer possible. Below is an example (reused from chapter 2) of three `it` blocks, each of which makes use of the same setup data: `Expression.parse("2x")`.

```
RSpec.describe "expression parser" do
  context "the expression involves multiplication without" \
          "an explicit operator" do
    it "assigns the multiplication operator to the root" do
      expression = Expression.parse("2x")
      expect(expression.root).to eq("*")
    end

    it "assigns the first operand to the left child" do
      expression = Expression.parse("2x")
      expect(expression.left_child).to eq(2)
    end

    it "assigns the second operand to the right child" do
      expression = Expression.parse("2x")
      expect(expression.right_child).to eq("x")
    end
  end
end
```

All three of these test cases use the same test data. The setup is duplicated three times but there's no reason or benefit to the duplication. We can DRY up the test and make it more DRY by moving the setup to the top of the test.

```
RSpec.describe "expression parser" do
  let!(:expression) { Expression.parse("2x") }

  context "the expression involves multiplication without" \
```

```
        "an explicit operator" do
    it "assigns the multiplication operator to the root" do
      expect(expression.root).to eq("*")
    end

    it "assigns the first operand to the left child" do
      expect(expression.left_child).to eq(2)
    end

    it "assigns the second operand to the right child" do
      expect(expression.right_child).to eq("x")
    end
  end
end
```

5.8 Helpers

There are the parts of a test that represent meaningful specifications and parts that simply carry out mechanical gruntwork.

This gruntwork can get noisy, distracting and repetitive. Because gruntwork code doesn't embody specifications, much of it can be moved out of a test without hurting the test's understandability. In fact, gruntwork code usually makes a test noisier and harder to understand, and so it *should* be moved to somewhere else. This is where test helpers can come into the picture.

5.8.1 Example: abstracting a noisy HTTP request

The test code below is a bit hard to understand. The meaning of the test is obscured by low-level details, specifically the details of making an HTTP request to the system logs API endpoint.

```
context "after log update occurs" do
  before do
    visit_build_tab("system_logs", job: original_job)
    navigate_to_job_tab(other_job)

    path = api_v1_job_system_logs_path(
      job_id: original_job.id,
      format: :json
    )
    uri = URI("#{Capybara.current_session.server_url}#{path}")

    http = Net::HTTP.new(uri.host, uri.port)
    http.use_ssl = uri.scheme == "https"
    request = Net::HTTP::Post.new(
      uri.request_uri,
```

```
      api_authorization_headers.merge(
        "Content-Type" => "text/plain"
      )
    )
    request.body = "new system log content"
    http.request(request)
  end

  it "does not show original job's system logs on" \
     "the other job's system logs tab" do
    expect(page).not_to have_content(original_job.system_logs)
  end

  it "shows the other job's system logs on" \
     "the other job's system logs tab" do
    expect(page).to have_content(other_job.system_logs)
  end
end
```

In order to make the test easier to understand, the HTTP request code can be moved into a helper. I chose the name SaturnAPIHelper since the project this code is from is called SaturnCI. I placed the helper code in spec/support/saturn_api_helper.rb.

```
require "net/http"

module SaturnAPIHelper
  include APIAuthenticationHelper

  def http_request(api_authorization_headers:, path:, body:)
    uri = URI("#{Capybara.current_session.server_url}#{path}")

    http = Net::HTTP.new(uri.host, uri.port)
    http.use_ssl = uri.scheme == "https"
    request = Net::HTTP::Post.new(
      uri.request_uri,
      api_authorization_headers.merge(
        "Content-Type" => "text/plain"
      )
    )
    request.body = body
    http.request(request)
  end
end
```

With this helper in place, the test can be written at a higher level of abstraction. In this newer version, there are fewer incidental details obscuring its meaning.

```
context "after log update occurs" do
  before do
    visit_build_tab("system_logs", job: original_job)
    navigate_to_job_tab(other_job)

    http_request(
      api_authorization_headers:,
      path: api_v1_job_system_logs_path(
        job_id: original_job.id,
        format: :json
      ),
      body: "new system log content"
    )
  end

  it "does not show original job's system logs on" \
     "the other job's system logs tab" do
    expect(page).not_to have_content(original_job.system_logs)
  end

  it "shows the other job's system logs on" \
     "the other job's system logs tab" do
    expect(page).to have_content(other_job.system_logs)
  end
end
```

This is an improvement, but actually the test can be written at a higher level of abstraction still. The authorization details, the request format and the exact path are all incidental details that the test could stand to live without.

```
module SaturnAPIHelper
  def system_log_http_request(job:, body:)
    http_request(
      api_authorization_headers:,
      path: api_v1_job_system_logs_path(
        job_id: job.id,
        format: :json
      ),
      body:
    )
  end

  def http_request(api_authorization_headers:, path:, body:)
    uri = URI("#{Capybara.current_session.server_url}#{path}")

    http = Net::HTTP.new(uri.host, uri.port)
    http.use_ssl = uri.scheme == "https"
    request = Net::HTTP::Post.new(
```

```
      uri.request_uri,
      api_authorization_headers.merge("Content-Type" => "text/plain")
    )
    request.body = body
    http.request(request)
  end
end
```

Now the test has a much higher signal-to-noise ratio.

```
context "after log update occurs" do
  before do
    visit_build_tab("system_logs", job: original_job)
    navigate_to_job_tab(other_job)

    system_log_http_request(
      job: original_job,
      body: "new system log content"
    )
  end

  it "does not show original job's system logs on" \
    "the other job's system logs tab" do
    expect(page).not_to have_content(original_job.system_logs)
  end

  it "shows the other job's system logs on" \
    "the other job's system logs tab" do
    expect(page).to have_content(other_job.system_logs)
  end
end
```

5.8.2 Test helpers and DRY

As we've seen elsewhere in the book, the DRY principle doesn't apply to test code in the same way that it applies to application code, since application code is *behavior* whereas test code is *specifications*.

Helpers aren't tests and they don't contain specifications. They simply help with gruntwork. Unlike test code, helper code *does* benefit from being DRY just like application code does.

5.9 Page objects

Like test helpers, page objects can add helpful abstraction to a test that contains too many incidental details. Page objects suffer from a somewhat misleading name. They're not meant to represent an entire page but rather one component of a page.

5.9.1   Example: BuildLink

Here's a test from a project of mine that I find pretty noisy, repetitive, and hard to understand.

```
require "rails_helper"

describe "Active link", type: :system do
  let!(:project) { create(:project) }

  let!(:build_1) do
    create(:build, :with_job, project: project)
  end

  let!(:build_2) do
    create(:build, :with_job, project: project)
  end

  before do
    user = create(:user)
    login_as(user, scope: :user)
    visit project_build_path(project, build_1)
  end

  context "link clicked" do
    it "sets that build to active" do
      click_on "build_link_#{build_2.id}"

      expect(
        find("#build_link_#{build_2.id}")[:class].split
      ).to include("active")
    end

    it "sets other builds to inactive" do
      click_on "build_link_#{build_2.id}"

      expect(
        find("#build_link_#{build_2.id}")[:class].split
      ).to include("active")

      click_on "build_link_#{build_1.id}"

      expect(
        find("#build_link_#{build_2.id}")[:class].split
      ).not_to include("active")
    end
  end
end
```

```
    context "page load" do
      it "sets the first build link to active" do
        expect(
          find("#build_link_#{build_1.id}")[:class].split
        ).to include("active")
      end
    end
end
```

The general pattern of #build_link_#{build_id} is repeated several times.
The snippet find("#build_link_#{build_1.id}")[:class].split is repeated
multiple times as well. Some of the test's gruntwork can be abstracted away using
a page object.

```
# spec/support/page_objects/build_link.rb

module PageObjects
  class BuildLink
    def initialize(page, build)
      @page = page
      @build = build
    end

    def click
      @page.click_on "build_link_#{@build.id}"
    end

    def active?
      css_classes.include?("active")
    end

    private

    def css_classes
      @page.find("#build_link_#{@build.id}")[:class].split
    end
  end
end
```

Below is how the page object can be used. Now that the noisy gruntwork can be
tucked away in a page object, the incidental details are gone, allowing the essential
meaning of the test to shine through, making the test much easier to understand.

```
require "rails_helper"

describe "Active link", type: :system do
  let!(:project) { create(:project) }
```

```
  let!(:build_1) do
    create(:build, :with_job, project: project)
  end

  let!(:build_2) do
    create(:build, :with_job, project: project)
  end

  let!(:build_link_1) do
    PageObjects::BuildLink.new(page, build_1)
  end

  let!(:build_link_2) do
    PageObjects::BuildLink.new(page, build_2)
  end

  before do
    user = create(:user)
    login_as(user, scope: :user)
    visit project_build_path(project, build_1)
  end

  context "link clicked" do
    it "sets that build to active" do
      build_link_2.click
      expect(build_link_2).to be_active
    end

    it "sets other builds to inactive" do
      build_link_2.click
      expect(build_link_2).to be_active

      build_link_1.click
      expect(build_link_2).not_to be_active
    end
  end

  context "page load" do
    it "sets the first build link to active" do
      expect(build_link_1).to be_active
    end
  end
end
```

Let's take a closer look at how to build page objects.

5.9.2   What's the scope of a page object?

Despite its name, a page object doesn't typically represent a page but rather a part of a page, such as a button or a text input. How broad or narrow a page object is is up to its designer's judgment.

5.9.3   Why do we need Capybara::Session?

The reason we can call methods like `find` and `click_on` in a system spec is because when these methods get called—or, more precisely, when these *messages* get *sent*—they get sent to an instance of `Capybara::Session`.

Our `BuildLink` object is a PORO (plain old Ruby object). It doesn't know anything about
`Capybara::Session`. But since `BuildLink` needs to use methods like `find` and `click_on`, we have to pass in an instance of `Capybara::Session`.

We can do this by passing to `BuildLink` the test's built-in page object, like so:

```
let!(:build_link_1) do
  PageObjects::BuildLink.new(page, build_1)
end
```

Then, whenever e.g. `click_on` needs to be used, it can be used by invoking it on the @page object, which again is an instance of `Capybara::Session`.

```
@page.click_on "build_link_#{@build.id}"
```

By the way, don't get confused by Capybara's `page` object and the design pattern called Page Object. They have nothing to do with each other other than that they both refer to objects and they both happen to have something to do with a page.

5.9.4   Predicate matchers

You might have noticed that in our test we were able to use a matcher called `be_active`.

```
it "sets other builds to inactive" do
  build_link_2.click
  expect(build_link_2).to be_active

  build_link_1.click
  expect(build_link_2).not_to be_active
end
```

This allows our test to read very naturally: "expect build link 2 to be active...expect build link 2 not to be active". How was this possible?

It's possible because any object that responds to a predicate method (i.e. a method ending in ? that returns true or false) can use that method as an RSpec matcher. In this case, the `BuildLink#active?` method translates to `be_active`.

```
def active?
  css_classes.include?("active")
end
```

As you gain experience with page objects, it's likely that you'll discover ways of designing your page objects that result in very clear and understandable tests.

5.10 Managing setup data

Most tests require some setup data. The more setup data there is, the harder it is to keep the test code understandable.

It's important for tests to be *deterministic*, meaning that they behave the same way every time. If a test is not deterministic, it may pass sometimes and fail sometimes, giving false negatives and causing numbness to legitimate failures.

A key ingredient in making a test deterministic is to start it in the same state every time. If a test is allowed to pollute its environment by changing e.g. environment variables, configuration settings or database data, then the test that runs after it will run in a "fouled" environment instead of a clean slate.

For this reason, Rails by default runs every test inside of a database transaction. Before the test finishes, the transaction gets aborted so that any data created inside the test never gets committed to the database. (There are other database cleaning strategies but transactions are the fastest and most common.)

Every piece of data that's in the database when a test starts—we'll call this data "background data"—has the potential to influence how the test behaves. Background data may also conflict or interfere with data created during the test. The less background data there is, the fewer headaches it can cause. The ideal amount of background data is zero.

Having said that, reality isn't always ideal, and sometimes a little background data is worth the price. I once built an electronic medical records system, for example, whose every feature depended on the presence of at least one physician. To meet this need I could have created a fresh physician for every test but that would have been mind-numbingly repetitive. Instead I chose to create a physician record as a piece of fixture data. This meant that I had to be conscious of the presence of a physician record in every test from then on, but between that and creating a physician in every test, it was the lesser of two evils.

When there's too much background data it can be maddening. I once worked on an application where every test started wiht a gigantic, inscrutable rat's nest of

background data. At any given stage in a test it was impossible to understand what
was in the database or why. Mysterious failures abounded. Writing tests was often
very painful. Worst of all, the test suite was so tightly coupled to the background
data that the problem was basically impossible to solve. Be cautious of adding too
much background data to your test suite. It comes with a price.

5.10.1 Anti-pattern: test setup conflation

Many tests combine all of their setup code at the top of the file. This makes the
setup harder to understand. Here's an example of such a test. Which values in
the setup data are needed for every test case in the file, and which values are only
needed for some?

```
RSpec.describe "User index" do
  let!(:user) { create(:user) }
  let!(:article) { create(:article, user: user) }
  let!(:other_article) { create(:article) }

  let!(:comment) do
    create(:comment, user: user, commentable: other_article)
  end

  let!(:comment2) do
    create(:comment, user: user, commentable: other_article)
  end

  let(:organization) { create(:organization) }

  context "when user is unauthorized" do
    before do
      visit "/#{user.username}"
    end

    context "when 1 article" do
      it "shows header", :aggregate_failures, js: true do
        within("h1.crayons-title") do
          expect(page).to have_content(user.name)
        end

        within(".profile-header__actions") do
          expect(page).to have_button(I18n.t("core.follow"))
        end
      end

      it "shows title", :aggregate_failures, js: true do
        expect(page).to have_title(
          "#{user.name} - #{Settings::Community.community_name}"
```

```
        )
      end

    it "shows articles", :aggregate_failures, js: true do
      within(".crayons-story") do
        expect(page).to have_content(article.title)
        expect(page).not_to have_content(other_article.title)
      end
    end

    it "shows comments locked cta", :aggregate_failures, js: true do
      within("#comments-locked-cta") do
        expect(page).to have_content(
          "Want to connect with #{user.name}?"
        )
      end
    end

    it "hides comments", :aggregate_failures, js: true do
      within("#substories") do
        expect(page).not_to have_content("Recent comments")
      end
    end
    end
  end
end
```

The answer to the question is: who knows! Surely they're not all needed for every test case above, but we can't say for sure which are needed and which aren't. Because we can't be sure, we can't safely move them out of the global setup. Because we can't safely change the global setup, each test case is in a state of tight coupling with the global setup. The test cases can't be easily understood and changed independently of other parts of the test. Understanding each test potentially requires understanding the whole global setup.

Below is an example of how this test, or at least part of it, could have been written. For the "shows header" test, I can't see any evidence that organization, other_article, comment or comment2 are needed. A user is clearly needed, since user.username is included in the path that gets visited, and one article is apparently needed, since the context says "when 1 article", but the rest can perhaps be dispensed with.

```
RSpec.describe "User index" do
  context "when user is unauthorized" do
    let!(:user) { create(:user) }

    before do
      visit "/#{user.username}"
```

```
    end

    context "when 1 article" do
      let!(:article) { create(:article, user: user) }

      it "shows header", :aggregate_failures, js: true do
        within("h1.crayons-title") do
          expect(page).to have_content(user.name)
        end
      end
    end
  end
end
```

Now this test case can be more easily understood on its own since we don't have to worry about whether the several other values from the global setup are involved in the test or not.

Bonus exercise: based on the other ideas we've seen in this chapter and throughout the book so far, what other possible improvements can you think of for this test? Do you think this test was written with a mindset of specification or verification? Why? Do you feel that everything in this test is at the appropriate level of abstraction? Is it easy to infer the test's high-level meaning? If you like, re-write the test on your own and see what improvements you can make over the original.

5.10.2   Naming

The following test has three setup values: `user`, `token` and `mismatch_token`. The meaning of `mismatch_token` is clear enough: it's apparently a token that mismatches in some way. But `token` has nothing in the name to give a clue as to what's significant about it.

```
RSpec.describe "User destroys their profile", js: true do
  let(:user) { create(:user) }
  let(:token) { SecureRandom.hex(10) }
  let(:mismatch_token) { SecureRandom.hex(10) }

  before do
    sign_in user
    allow(Honeycomb).to receive(:add_field)
  end

  it "requests self-destroy" do
    visit "/settings/account"

    allow(Users::RequestDestroy)
      .to receive(:call)
```

```
      .and_call_original

    click_button "Delete Account"

    expect(Users::RequestDestroy)
      .to have_received(:call)
      .with(user)
  end

  it "displays a detailed error message when user not logged in" do
    sign_out user
    visit "/users/confirm_destroy/#{token}"
    expect(page).to have_text(
      "You must be logged in to proceed with account deletion."
    )
  end

  it "displays a detailed error message when user token invalid" do
    visit "/users/confirm_destroy/#{token}"
    expect(page).to have_text(
      "Your token has expired, please request a new one."
    )
  end

  it "raises a 'Not Found' error if there is a token mismatch" do
    visit "/settings/account"
    click_button "Delete Account"
    allow(Rails.cache).to receive(:read).and_return(token)
    expect do
      get user_confirm_destroy_path(token: mismatch_token)
    end.to raise_error(ActionController::RoutingError)
  end

  it "destroys an account" do
    allow(Rails.cache).to receive(:read).and_return(token)
    visit "/users/confirm_destroy/#{token}"
    fill_in "delete__account__username__field", with: user.username

    fill_in(
      "delete__account__verification__field",
      with: "delete my account"
    )

    sidekiq_assert_enqueued_with(job: Users::DeleteWorker) do
      click_button "Delete account"
    end
  end
end
end
```

From reading the test we can see that `token` is apparently a valid token. Perhaps `valid_token` would be a clearer name.

```
RSpec.describe "User destroys their profile", js: true do
  let(:user) { create(:user) }
  let(:valid_token) { SecureRandom.hex(10) }
  let(:mismatch_token) { SecureRandom.hex(10) }
end
```

A good rule of thumb for naming is "call things what they are". This rule may sound obvious, but how many times have your encountered a variable, method, class or database table that's named according to something other than what it actually is?

Clear naming is worth a significant time investment. I'd rather sweat over the name of an important entity for three days than give it a name that's misleading. Because code is read many more times than it's written, the cost of a poor name is often many times more than the cost "saved" by skipping the effort of giving it a clear name. You don't always have to get the name right on the first try, but it pays to try to get the name right before it gets deeply baked into the system and becomes too expensive to change.

5.11 One topic per test

Some testers believe that each test should have just one assertion. Others believe this rule is hogwash, and that a test should have as many assertions as it needs. Still others believe that one assertion per test is a good target, but that it shouldn't be a strictly-enforced rule. I happen to think that all these attitudes focus on the wrong thing. The significant thing about a test is not how many *assertions* it contains but rather how many *topics* it contains.

A test with just one topic—a test that's only "about" one thing—is going to be easier to understand than a test that conflates multiple topics. Below is a piece of code that inappropriately combines several different ideas into a single test.

```
RSpec.describe 'Post interactions', type: :system do
  let(:user) { create(:user) }

  before do
    driven_by(:rack_test)
    sign_in user

    create(
      :post,
      title: 'First Post',
      content: 'This is the first post.',
      user: user
```

```
    )

    create(
      :post,
      title: 'Second Post',
      content: 'This is the second post.',
      user: user
    )
  end

  it 'creates, edits, comments on, and likes a post' do
    visit root_path
    expect(page).to have_content('First Post')
    expect(page).to have_content('Second Post')
    expect(page).to have_selector(:link_or_button, 'Your Profile')

    click_on 'New Post'
    fill_in 'Title', with: 'Third Post'
    fill_in 'Content', with: 'This is the third post.'
    click_on 'Submit'
    expect(page).to have_content('Post was successfully created')
    expect(page).to have_content('Third Post')

    click_on 'Edit', match: :first
    fill_in 'Content', with: 'This is an edited post.'
    click_on 'Submit'
    expect(page).to have_content('Post was successfully updated')
    expect(page).to have_content('This is an edited post.')

    fill_in 'Comment', with: 'Great post!'
    click_on 'Add Comment'
    expect(page).to have_content('Comment was successfully added')
    expect(page).to have_content('Great post!')

    click_on 'Like'
    expect(page).to have_content('You liked this post')

    click_on 'Logout'
    expect(page).to have_content('Signed out successfully')

    visit user_profile_path(user)
    expect(page).to have_content(user.email)
    expect(page).to have_content('Your Posts')
    expect(page).to have_link('Edit Profile')
  end
end
```

Long, incoherent tests like this tend to be hard to understand and hard to debug when things go wrong. It would be better if each specification is put into its own test.

It's common for developers to stuff several assertions into one test out of a desire for performance efficiency, especially in system specs, which are expensive to run. I think this is usually a false economy. Yes, a performance benefit is achieved, but at the expense of understandability. The savings in CPU time is paid for by engineer time. We of course know which of the two is more expensive.

5.12   The phases of a test

Every test has four phases: setup, exercise, assertion and teardown. In Rails, the teardown usually happens automatically, so we only need to think about the setup, exercise and assertion steps. These three steps are also sometimes known as *arrange, act, assert.*

Let's look at a couple examples. In the test below, see if you can identify the setup, exercise and assertion phases.

```
RSpec.describe "one failing job" do
  let!(:build) { create(:build) }

  describe "build status" do
    it "gets set to 'Failed'" do
      passing_job.finish!
      failing_job.finish!
      expect(build.reload.cached_status).to eq("Failed")
    end
  end
end
```

The setup phase is the creation of the build on the second line of the test. The exercise phase, part of what makes the test unique and meaningful, is the finishing of one passing job and one failing job. Lastly, the assertion of course is the step where we expect the build's `cached_status` to be "Failed".

Here's another example. As with the example above, try to identify the setup, exercise and assertion phases.

```
RSpec.describe "test reports", type: :request do
  describe "POST /api/v1/jobs/:id/test_reports" do
    let!(:job) { create(:job) }

    it "adds a report to a job" do
      post(
        api_v1_job_test_reports_path(job_id: job.id),
        params: "test report content",
        headers: api_authorization_headers.merge(
```

```
        { "CONTENT_TYPE" => "text/plain" }
      )
    )

    expect(job.reload.test_report).to eq("test report content")
  end
end
end
```

The setup is where the job gets created. The exercise is the POST request to the endpoint that updates a job's test report. Finally, the test asserts that the job's test report has indeed been updated.

Before we finish let's take a look at an anti-example, a case where the setup, exercise and assertion phases are a bit less clearly separated.

```
RSpec.describe Tweet, :vcr do
  let(:tweet_id) { "1018911886862057472" }
  let(:tweet_reply_id) { "1242938461784608770" }
  let(:retweet_id) { "1262395854469677058" }

  describe ".find_or_fetch" do
    context "when retrieving a tweet", vcr: {
      cassette_name: "twitter_client_status_extended"
    } do
      it "saves the proper status ID and text" do
        tweet = described_class.find_or_fetch(tweet_id)

        status = tweet.full_fetched_object_serialized

        expect(tweet.text).to eq(status[:full_text])
        expect(tweet.twitter_id_code).to eq(status[:id_str])
      end
    end
  end
end
```

The three tweet ids that are created in the beginning of the test are clearly part of a setup phase. What about `tweet` and `status` inside of the test case itself? Those look like they might be setup data as well. This test probably would have been a bit clearer if these values were neatly separated from the assertions.

Incidentally, the example above also highlights the benefits of a) limiting each test to one topic and b) writing tests in the form of specifications, not verifications. The test asserts that `.find_or_fetch` "saves the proper status ID and text", but it doesn't show what proper *means*. The conflation of status ID and status text also forces the reader to think of multiple aspects of the system's behavior simultaneously instead of being able to focus on each behavior individually.

Creating a clear separation among the three phases of a test is one of the many small improvements that makes a test easier to understand. When combined with other readability tactics, it makes a dramatic difference in the quality of the tests.

5.13   Organizing your test suite

As we saw at the beginning of this chapter, a test suite, when thought of as a structured set of behavior specifications, can serve as the backbone of a system's design.

The files and folders in a test suite should be laid out in an orderly and logical fashion so that when one needs to find something, it can be found easily. When you're working with a piece of model code, for example, and you want to see the tests for it, how do you know where to look? That model code may be covered by a model spec, request spec, system spec, a combination, or no test at all. How can you easily find the code's test(s) when you don't know exactly what you're looking for?

For Rails apps that use RSpec, it's customary for the spec directory to be subdivided into folders for each test type: `models`, `requests`, `system` and so on. Virtually all Rails apps use this structure because it's the default that the RSpec framework gives us. Very few developers stop to question whether this directory structure makes logical sense.

5.13.1   Organizing tests by domain concept

Instead of organizing tests by test type, which in a sense is an incidental detail, I find it more logical to organize my tests by domain concept. This way, when I'm working with, for example, a piece of billing-related code which lives in the `billing` namespace, I know I can find its test somewhere in the `spec/billing` folder. I don't have to know whether I'm looking for a model spec, system spec or something else, nor do I have to individually search through `spec/models/billing`, `spec/system/billing` and any other folders that could potentially contain billing-related tests.

Each folder in a test suite can be thought of as having two dimensions: to what domain concept it belongs and to what type of test it pertains. For example, a folder called `spec/system/billing` would belong to the *billing* domain concept and pertain to the *system* test type. Because of this two-dimensional aspect of test folders, one can imagine plotting folders in a two-dimensional table, as shown below. Each row represents a test type and each column represents a domain concept.

Above is represented the customary RSpec directory structure, where the test type is the "primary index" and the domain concept is the "secondary index". Under this structure, a system spec for creating an invoice, for example, may be located at `spec/system/billing/create_invoice_spec.rb`. In the table below, the axes are flipped: domain concept is the primary index and test type is the sec-

	billing	schedule	clinical
models	models/billing	models/schedule	models/clinical
requests	requests/billing	requests/schedule	requests/clinical
system	system/billing	system/schedule	system/clinical

Table 5.1: The customary RSpec directory structure: test type is primary index

ondary index. Under this scheme the invoice-creation spec would instead be located at `spec/billing/system/create_invoice_spec.rb`. (Note the change from `system/billing` to `billing/system`.)

	models	requests	system
billing	billing/models	billing/requests	billing/system
schedule	schedule/models	schedule/requests	schedule/system
clinical	clinical/models	clinical/requests	clinical/system

Table 5.2: My preferred RSpec directory structure: domain concept is primary index

Given how different it is from the customary way of organizing tests, this way of organizing tests might seem strange to you, even heretical. But the only reason the customary way of organizing test files feels so familiar and natural is because it's so common, not because it's logical.

You might wonder: but what about convention? Rails is known for its wonderful convention-over-configuration philosophy. Doesn't this deviation break that concept? That's a good question. Let's talk about it.

5.13.2 What about convention?

The organization of the `spec` folder in a test suite is neither a part of Rails nor a convention. Remember, RSpec is aware of your Rails app, but your Rails app knows nothing of RSpec. Rails conventions always involve a functional connection, such as when, for example, visiting a route like `invoices/new` resolves to the `InvoicesController#new` controller action, for example. Folders and files inside of `spec` have no functional connection to anything. A file called `spec/billing/invoice_spec.rb` could just as easily be called `spec/banana/hubcap_spec.rb` and it would work just the same. Organizing RSpec files according to test type is a *custom*, not a convention.

5.13.3   Catching regressions more efficiently

In addition to making tests easier to find, the index-by-domain-concept structure also makes local regression testing easier and more efficient. When a change is made to a certain area, any regression that that change introduces is most likely to lie close to the place the change was made. The easier it is to catch the regression, the less cost the regression will incur.

As far as ways to catch a regression go, waiting for the entire test suite to run on CI is a pretty inefficient way to do it. That's like misplacing your phone, then searching your entire house in random order, even though your phone was sitting right next to you on the table right from the start. It would have been much more efficient to search the area immediately surrounding you, then search the whole kitchen, then whatever room you were hanging out in just before that, and so on.

When tests are organized by domain concept, the search for regressions can be conducted much more logically and efficiently.[3] Once you get
`spec/schedule/appointments/system/cancel_appointment_spec.rb` passing, for example, you can then locally run all the tests in the parent folder, `spec/schedule/appointments`. If all those tests pass, you can run everything in `spec/schedule`. If all those tests pass, you can push everything up to CI to let the whole test suite run. This is analogous to searching for your phone starting with the places you were most likely to have left it, rather than immediately searching the whole house in random order. When this approach is used, regressions, when they inevitably occur, tend to be caught more quickly, and ergo can be fixed less expensively.

With enough time and effort, any knucklehead can write tests that function as desired. It takes a higher level of thought to write tests that can not only function but be easily understood and maintained. In the best scenario, your test suite can serve as the authoritative documentation for your system, guiding you to the behavior you want to find at any given moment, and dramatically reducing the system's cost of ownership.

---

[3]In addition to organizing tests in folders by domain concept, another way to run tests grouped by domain concept is to use RSpec's tagging feature. However, this approach has what I consider a dealbreaking weakness. The practice can be successful if and only if every developer has the discipline and presence of mind to appropriately tag every test in the test suite. In my opinion, this is an unrealistic expectation.

Chapter 6

Duplication in test code

You may have heard that duplication is more acceptable in test code than in application code. Is this true? If so, why? And if it's true that duplication is to be avoided in general, why is that true? And for that matter, what exactly *is* duplication?

It's commonly believed that duplication is code that appears in two or more places. But this is actually mistaken. **Duplication is when there's a single *behavior* that's specified in two or more places**.

Just because two identical pieces of code are present doesn't necessarily mean duplication exists. And just because there are no two identical pieces of code present doesn't mean there's no duplication.

Two pieces of code could happen to be identical, but if they actually serve different purposes and lead separate lives, then they don't represent the same behavior, and they don't constitute duplication. To "DRY up" these identical-looking pieces of code would create new problems, like handcuffing two people together who need to walk in two different directions.

On the other hand, it's possible for a single behavior to be represented in a codebase but with non-identical code. The way to tell if two pieces of code are duplicative isn't to see if their code matches. The question that determines duplication is: if I changed one piece of code in order to meet a new requirement, would it be logically necessary to update the other piece of code the same way? If so, then the two pieces of code are probably duplicates of each other, even if their behavior is not achieved using the same exact syntax.

6.1   The costs and risks of duplication

The main reason duplication is bad is because it leaves a program susceptible to developing logical inconsistencies. If a behavior is expressed in two different places in a program, and one of them accidentally doesn't match the other, then the deviating behavior is necessarily wrong. (Or if the deviating behavior happens to still meet its requirements, it only does so by accident.)

Another reason duplication can be bad is because it can pose an extra mainte-nance burden. It takes longer, and requires more mental energy, to apply a change to two areas of code instead of just one. Sometimes the additional maintenance cost is significant. But not all instances of duplication are equally bad. Some kinds of duplication are riskier than others.

6.2   What determines how risky duplication is

There are three factors that determine the degree of risk posed by an instance of duplication: 1) how easily noticeable the duplication is, 2) how much extra main-tenance overhead the presence of the duplication incurs, and 3) how much "traffic" that area receives, i.e. how frequently that area of code needs to be changed or understood. Let's look at each of these factors more closely.

6.2.1   Noticeability

If there's a piece of behavior that's specified twice in the codebase, but the two pieces of code are only separated by one line, then the problem is very noticeable and so there's not a big risk. If someone updates one of the copies of the behavior to meet a new requirement, they're very unlikely to miss updating the other one. We might call this the **proximity factor**.

If two pieces of duplicated behavior appear in different files in different areas of the application, then a "miss" is much more likely to occur, and therefore the duplication poses a larger risk.

Another quality that makes the noticeability of duplication easier is similarity. If two pieces of code *look* very similar, then their duplicity is more likely to be noticed than if the two pieces of code don't look the same. You might call this the **similarity factor**.

If for an instance of duplication the proximity factor is bad (the pieces of dupli-cated code are at a great distance from each other) and/or if the similarity factor is bad (the duplication is obscured by the pieces of duplicated code not being similar enough to appear obviously duplicative) then it means the instance of duplication is riskier.

6.2.2   Maintenance overhead

Some instances of duplication are easier to live with than others. Two short lines of very similar code, located right next to each other, are very easy to keep in agreement with each other. Other forms of duplication can be much more deeply baked into the system and can cause a much bigger headache.

For example, if a piece of duplication exists as part of the database schema, that's a much higher maintenance cost than a small duplication in code. Instances of duplication that are large and aren't represented by identical code can also be costly to maintain because, in those cases, you can't just type the same thing twice, you have to perform a potentially expensive translation step in your head.

6.2.3 Traffic level

When considering how much a piece of problematic code costs, it's worth considering *when* that cost is incurred. When a piece of bad code incurs a cost, we might think of this as analogous to paying a toll on a toll road.

One tollway is when a piece of code is changed. The more frequently the code is changed, the more of a toll it's going to incur, and so the bigger a problem it is.

Another tollway is when a piece of code needs to be understood as a prerequisite to understanding a different piece of code. Every codebase has "leaf code" and "branch code". If a piece of code is leaf code, as in nothing depends on it, then we can often afford for that code to be pretty bad and it doesn't matter. Branch code, on the other hand, gets heavy intellectual traffic, and so incurs a higher toll, and so is a bigger problem.

6.3 How to decide whether to DRY up a piece of code

The way to decide whether or not to DRY up a piece of duplication is pretty simple, although it's not always easy. There are two factors to consider.

6.3.1 Severity

If a piece of duplication is "severe"—i.e. it has low noticeability, poses high maintenance overhead, and/or has a high traffic level—then those all add weight to the argument that the duplication should be cleaned up.

6.3.2 Quality of alternative

Just because a piece of duplication costs something doesn't automatically mean that the de-duplicated version costs less. It doesn't happen very often, but sometimes a de-duplication unavoidably results in code that's so generalized that it's virtually impossible to understand. In these cases, the duplicated version may be the lesser of two evils.

But be careful to make the distinction between "this code can't be de-duplicated without making it worse" and *"this particular attempt* to de-duplicate this code made it worse". Like all refactoring projects, sometimes you just need to try a few times before you land on something you're happy with. And sometimes you just need to be careful not to go overboard.

6.4   The popular guidelines around duplication, and why they make little sense

It currently seems to be fashionable to hold the belief that developers apply DRY (Don't Repeat Yourself) too eagerly. This hasn't been my experience. The opposite has been my experience.

Claims that developers apply DRY too eagerly are often accompanied by advice to follow WET ("write everything twice") or the "rule of three", or to heed the fact that "duplication is cheaper than the wrong abstraction". Here's why I think these popular guidelines make little sense.

6.4.1   Rule of three/"write everything twice"

When I'm deciding whether to DRY up a duplication, I ask myself: how severe is this instance of duplication? Are we able to come up with a fix that's better than the duplicated version and not worse?

My criteria do not include "does the duplication appear three times"? Whether a piece of behavior is duplicated three times or just two is completely orthogonal to how much risk is posed by that instance of duplication.

Imagine, for example, a piece of duplication in the form of three very simple and nearly-identical lines, grouped together in a single file. The file is an unimportant one which only gets touched a couple times a year, and no one needs to understand that piece of code as a prerequisite to understanding anything else.

Now imagine another piece of duplication. The duplication appears in only two places, but the places are distant from each other and therefore the duplication is hard to notice. The two places where the duplicated behavior appear are expressed differently enough that the code would elude detection by a code quality tool or a manual human search. The behavior is a vitally central and important one. It doesn't get changed often enough that it stays at the top of everyone's mind, but it gets changed often enough that there are lots of opportunities for divergences to arise. And the two places the behavior appears are brutally painful to keep in sync.

Given this scenario, why on earth would I choose to fix the triple-duplicate and leave the double-duplicate alone?

6.4.2   "Duplication is cheaper than the wrong abstraction"

This statement is repeated very frequently in the Ruby community, usually to discourage people from applying the DRY principle too eagerly.

I wish we would think about this statement more deeply. Why are we setting up such a strong a connection between duplication and abstractions? I think it's a non-sequitur. And why are we imagining such a strong danger of creating the *wrong* abstraction? Do we not trust ourselves to DRY up a piece of code and end up with something *good*? And again, why does the result of our de-duplicating have to be an *abstraction*? It doesn't. Not every piece of code is an abstraction.

If we take out the word "abstraction" then the sentiment that remains is "duplicated code is better than a de-duplicated version that's even worse". In which case I of course agree, but the statement is so banal that it's hardly worth making. I think the statement "duplication is cheaper than the wrong abstraction" is not only devoid of any useful meaning but actively misleading. Let's stop repeating it.

6.5 Why duplication is more acceptable in tests

Duplication is subject to a different set of principles in test code than in application code. Why is this?

6.5.1 Incorrect reasons why duplication is more acceptable in tests

First let's examine the answers that are commonly given to this question, but which are wrong.

"Duplication in test code can be clearer than the DRY version"

It's true that duplication in test code can be clearer than the DRY version. But duplication in *application* code can be clearer than the DRY version too. So if duplicating code can make it clearer, why not favor duplication in application code to the same exact degree as in test code? This answer doesn't actually answer the question. The question is specifically about the *difference* between duplication in test code and application code.

"Duplication isn't actually that bad."

This answer also misses the point. The question isn't whether duplication is bad or not. The question is about the *relative* cost of duplication in application code versus test code.

So, what's the real difference?

6.5.2 The real difference between duplication in test code and application code

Duplication, again, is when one behavior is expressed in two or more places. The difference between test code and application code is that test code doesn't contain **behaviors**. All the behaviors are in the application code. The purpose of the test code is to **specify** the behaviors of the application code.

What in the codebase determines whether the application code is correct? The tests. If the application code passes its tests (i.e. its specifications), then the application code is correct. What in the code determines whether the tests (specifications) are correct? Nothing! The program's specifications come entirely from outside the program.

This means that whatever the tests specify is, by definition, correct. If we have two tests containing the same code and one of the tests changes, it does not always logically follow that the other test needs to be updated to match. This is different from duplicated application code. If a piece of behavior is duplicated in two places in the application code and one piece of behavior gets changed, it *does* always logically follow that the other piece of behavior needs to get updated to match. (Otherwise it wouldn't be in instance of duplication.) This difference is the real reason why duplication is more acceptable in test code than in application code.

Chapter 7

Mocks and stubs

Sports are sometimes like programming. A Friday night high school football game, for example, where a crowd is watching and the outcome of the game has material consequences, is a bit like, say, a production e-commerce system running during a big holiday sale. A football scrimmage, where a single team splits into two different "teams" to play a practice game with no spectators, is like a test environment.

In a scrimmage, why is the "test environment" the way it is? There's no reason why practice games absolutely have to happen this way. In theory, instead of splitting itself in two, a football team could practice against a neighboring town's team. It would certainly make for a more realistic game. In fact, practice games could even happen in front of a crowd. You could even bring in the high school band!

There are certain downsides to mimicking a "production environment" this closely, of course. Neither team is likely want to incur the expense (in time and money) of traveling to the other team's location to play the practice game. It would also be weird to bring in spectators. If nothing else, the spectators may get confused about what was a real game and what was a practice game. And from the perspective of practicing football, allowing the band to play would simply waste the players' time. A test environment that closely matches a production environment is often not worth what it costs.

There are yet more benefits to doing a scrimmage instead of playing an actual opposing team. If the "other team" is your own guys, then you have full control over the environment. You can tell the other team to perform such-and-such play so that you can practice defending against that specific play.[1] Playing against yourself also avoids "polluting the environment". If you play against a real team repeatedly, then that team may learn enough about your team's playing that future practices they'll play against you differently, compromising the validity and effectiveness of the practice sessions. Playing against yourself carries no such risk.

---

[1] Disclaimer: I have played football approximately zero times, and I know nothing about sports. My examples may be unrealistic.

7.1   What's a stub?

When a football team plays a scrimmage, they're "stubbing" the opposing team by using their own players. They use a fake team because, as we've seen, using a real team would incur too many expenses or side effects.

Similarly, in programming, a *stub* is a stand-in for a piece of application behavior which would, in a test, incur unacceptable expenses or side effects. Later in this chapter we'll see several examples of this.

7.2   What's a mock?

A *mock object* is like an undercover boss. The corporate headquarters of a fast food restaurant sends the undercover boss, whom we'll call Mr. Boss, into a certain location. Mr. Boss orders, let's say, a hamburger, fries and a Coke.

After the restaurant visit, Mr. Boss's boss interrogates him. "Did you receive the hamburger you ordered?" she asks. "Did you receive the fries you ordered?" and so on. If any of these "assertions" returns false, that particular test fails.

Mr. Boss is a mock object. He isn't exactly a real customer; he's a fake customer who behaves just like a customer, but with the added characteristic that he records his experiences and makes himself available for interrogation. Later in this chapter we'll see some examples of mock objects.

7.3   Testing third-party interactions using stubs

When testing a scenario that involves a third-party service, the third-party service is like an opposing football team. It wouldn't be appropriate to get them involved if we're not doing something real.

7.3.1   The downsides of using live services

In principle we could test third-party interactions by actually hitting live services. If our application uses the Stripe API, for example, then our tests could hit the Stripe API in test mode. The upside to this approach is that it provides a very realistic environment. We could hardly come closer to mimicking the way the system will behave in production. There are downsides to this approach, however.

Loss of determinism

By using live services, we lose some valuable control over our tests. For one, we can't control whether a service will always be available, or even if the network that connects us to the service will be available. This means that our tests will potentially be *non-deterministic*. Determinism is the property of always behaving the same way given the same starting conditions. Tests that involve third-party services may behave one way on some runs and another way on other runs even though the starting conditions were the same. If our tests are non-deterministic (also called *flaky*—see chapter 16) then they will give false negatives and become unreliable.

Limited ability to control test scenarios

When writing tests that involve third-party services, it's often desirable to cover certain scenarios such as when the service returns a valid response, when the service returns a graceful error response, and when the server returns a 500 error. A 500 response, by definition, is only returned when a system enters an error state. Unless we're "lucky" and can manipulate the third-party system into breaking and responding with a 500, creating this scenario is impossible.

Side effects

Often, unfortunately, service providers don't provide any sort of test or sandbox environment. All work must be done in the production environment. (It's crazy that this is ever the case but that's the world we live in.) In these cases it's obviously undesirable to let the tests create data in the production environment.

Using live services can also cause rate-limiting, causing the tests to eventually flake once requests start failing due to rate limits, and also preventing real production requests from being completed successfully.

Because of side effects, using live services makes it hard or impossible to make our tests each start in a known state. If a test doesn't always start in the same known state, it's susceptible to flakiness.

7.3.2 Stubbing services

Stubbing third-party services avoids the problems that come with using live services. When services are stubbed, our tests can be deterministic, we can control our test scenarios and we don't have to worry about introducing side effects.

What exactly is stubbing? It's the practice of replacing one piece of behavior with another. It's like laying a plank across a stream. Without the plank, we would have to climb down the stream bank, wade through the icy water and then climb up the bank on the other side. If we were specifically trying to test our toughness, this might be a good exercise. But if we're just trying to get from one place to another and the stream is nothing but an obstacle, it's better to lay down our plank so we can just get across and get on with our business.

Coming up with good tests

What exactly does it mean to write a test for a piece of behavior that involves a third-party interaction? A common mistake is to write tests that "make sure the API gets called" and to "make sure the right results get returned". I've even seen tests that stub an API and then turn right back around and check the fake results that the stub returns. Nothing could be more pointless.

Remember that testing is about specification, not verification. The task isn't to "make sure the code worked" but rather to specify *how* the code should work. (See chapter 1 for a refresher.) And remember, the behavior we're interested in testing—indeed, the only behavior we *can* test—is the behavior of our own system, not the behavior of the third-party service. Let's take a look at how we can come up with specifications for behaviors that involve third-party services.

Devising specifications for third-party service interaction

Usually, the most interesting part of our system's behavior is the way our system handles the third party service's *response*. In the happy path scenario when the service returns a 200 response, our system should behave one way. When the service returns a certain kind of error, our system should behave another way. To come up with our tests, we can list all the relevant scenarios we can think of and how we would expect our system to behave under those scenarios.

Our system's *request* to the third-party service is also relevant, but the behavior that generates the request usually has fewer moving parts and so doesn't call for as many tests as the response.

7.4   Third-party interaction example: Stripe payment

Like we just saw, there are times when a third-party service interaction is just simply in the way of the thing we really want to test. Other times, the third-party interaction itself is precisely what we're interested in. This example is of that type.

In this example we're interested in two scenarios: one where a payment attempt is made using a valid card and another where a payment attempt is made using an expired card. When a valid card is used, the customer's order balance should be reduced by however much the payment was. When an invalid card is used, the order balance should of course stay the same since the payment was not possible. Note that we're specifically focusing on what happens to the *order balance* under these two scenarios.

1. **Making a payment attempt using a valid card**

    (a) When an order exists for $50 and a $50 payment is attempted on that order using a **valid** card, **the order's balance becomes $0**.

2. **Making a payment attempt using an expired card**

   (a) When an order exists for $50 and a $50 payment is attempted on that order using an **expired** card, **the order's balance stays at $50**.

Let's write some tests, starting with the valid card scenario.

7.4.1   Test for paying with a valid card

Before we write the actual test code, let's think in more detail about what the actual test steps should be. For background, let's assume the existence of an OrderPayment.create method that looks like this.

```
class OrderPayment
  def self.create(order:, stripe_token:, amount_cents:)
    stripe_charge = Stripe::Charge.create(
      amount: amount_cents,
      source: stripe_token
    )

    return unless stripe_charge.paid

    order.payments << Payment.create!(amount_cents:)
  end
end
```

How would we write a test that asserts that a successful payment brings the order's balance from $50 to $0?

1. If the premise of the test is that we're starting with an order for $50, we'll have to create that order. So the first step will be to create an order with a balance of $50.

2. Next we'll have to make the payment attempt. As you can see above, the Stripe::Charge.create method from the Stripe SDK takes an amount and something called a stripe_token. The token is a unique identifier that allows us to use whatever credit card information the user entered but without having to get our hands dirty by actually handling the credit card information ourselves. Since we won't be hitting the actual Stripe API, it doesn't matter what value we use for stripe_token. So we can attempt the payment by calling OrderPayment.create with the order from step 1, an amount of $50, and an arbitrary string for stripe_token.

3. Since we expect the payment attempt to be successful, we should make an assertion that the order balance was reduced from $50 to $0.

Here's how the code for such a test might look.

```
RSpec.describe OrderPayment do
  let!(:order) { create(:order, amount_cents: 5000) }

  context "valid card" do
    it "brings the order balance to $0" do
      OrderPayment.create(
        order: order,
        amount_cents: 5000,
        stripe_token: "some_token"
      )

      expect(order.reload.balance_cents).to eq(0)
    end
  end
end
```

If we were to run this test as-is, it wouldn't work. Since we haven't stubbed anything yet, this test would simply make a request to the real Stripe API. Let's see how we can stub the Stripe API call so this test will behave how we need it to.

How to stub the Stripe response using allow

Remember that whether a payment gets created hinges on whether stripe_charge.paid returns true or not.

```
class OrderPayment
  def self.create(order:, stripe_token:, amount_cents:)
    stripe_charge = Stripe::Charge.create(
      amount: amount_cents,
      source: stripe_token
    )

    # If stripe_charge.paid is false, the method will
    # return here and no order will be created
    return unless stripe_charge.paid

    order.payments << Payment.create!(amount_cents:)
  end
end
```

Somehow, we have to stub the Stripe::Charge.create method such that it will return an object that responds to a message called paid and responds with true. How can we do this?

Let's start with a smaller question: how, in general, can we create an object that responds to a message called paid and returns true? There are ways of doing it using RSpec features, but, just to show you that there's no magic involved, let's look at an example using Ruby's OpenStruct library.

```
:001 > require "ostruct"
=> true
:002 > stripe_charge_response = OpenStruct.new(paid: true)
=> #<OpenStruct paid=true>
:003 > stripe_charge_response.paid
=> true
:004 >
```

Connecting this OpenStruct idea with RSpec's stubbing features, here's how we can stub Stripe::Charge.create to return an object that responds to paid with true.

```
stripe_charge_response = OpenStruct.new(paid: true)

allow(Stripe::Charge)
  .to receive(:create)
  .and_return(stripe_charge_response)
```

Now when Stripe::Charge.create is called, its return value will be an object that responds to paid with true.

Finally, here's how we can insert our stubbing code into our test to achieve the desired behavior.

```
RSpec.describe OrderPayment do
  let!(:order) { create(:order, amount_cents: 5000) }

  context "valid card" do
    before do
      stripe_charge_response = OpenStruct.new(paid: true)

      allow(Stripe::Charge)
        .to receive(:create)
        .and_return(stripe_charge_response)
    end

    it "brings the order balance to $0" do
      OrderPayment.create(
        order: order,
        amount_cents: 5000,
        stripe_token: "tok_visa"
      )

      expect(order.reload.balance_cents).to eq(0)
    end
  end
end
```

By stubbing the Stripe API response, we can test the interesting parts of our code without having to incur the unacceptable side effects that would come from hitting the live Stripe API.

7.4.2   Test for paying with an invalid card

Here's the specification for attempting to make a payment using an expired card.

> When an order exists for $50 and a $50 payment is attempted on that order using an **expired** card, **the order's balance stays at $50.**

Here's what the test for this might look like. There are only two differences between this test and the test for paying with a valid card. First, the Stripe charge response returns `false` instead of `true`, in order to signify a failed payment attempt. Second, instead of expecting the order balance to have fallen from $50 to $0, we expect the failed payment attempt not to have changed the order balance.

```
RSpec.describe OrderPayment do
  let!(:order) { create(:order, amount_cents: 5000) }

  context "valid card" do
    before do
      stripe_charge_response = OpenStruct.new(paid: true)

      allow(Stripe::Charge)
        .to receive(:create)
        .and_return(stripe_charge_response)
    end

    it "brings the order balance to $0" do
      OrderPayment.create(
        order: order,
        amount_cents: 5000,
        stripe_token: "tok_visa"
      )

      expect(order.reload.balance_cents).to eq(0)
    end
  end

  context "invalid card" do
    before do
      stripe_charge_response = OpenStruct.new(paid: false)

      allow(Stripe::Charge)
        .to receive(:create)
        .and_return(stripe_charge_response)
```

```
    end

    it "keeps the order balance at $50" do
      OrderPayment.create(
        order: order,
        amount_cents: 5000,
        stripe_token: "tok_visa"
      )

      expect(order.reload.balance_cents).to eq(50)
    end
  end
end
```

Remember that the behavior we're interested in is what happens *after* the Stripe response is received. If the response indicates success, we create a payment record and add it to the order. If the response indicates failure, we do nothing. Like the football scrimmage team from earlier in the chapter, stubbing the Stripe API response has allowed us to test our program's behavior without incurring the expense and side effects of an external dependency.

7.5   Third-party interaction example: GitHub token

Sometimes a third-party service is merely in the way. In these cases we want to stub the service interaction just so we don't have to deal with it. The following example is such a case.

The following API endpoint generates a GitHub token and then sends a response containing the token. There's obviously not a lot of behavior here in this controller to test, but it would be good to have at least one test covering this controller so we know that it behaves as expected.

```
module API
  module V1
    class GitHubTokensController < APIController
      def create
        render plain: GitHubToken.generate(
          params[:github_installation_id]
        )
      end
    end
  end
end
```

If we wanted to write a request spec for this API endpoint, how would we do it? Perhaps we would send a POST request to the route that matches the controller

and then assert that the response body contains a token. Below is a possible implementation of such a test.

```
require "rails_helper"
include APIAuthenticationHelper

RSpec.describe "GitHub tokens", type: :request do
  describe "POST /api/v1/github_tokens" do
    it "returns a token" do
      post(
        api_v1_github_tokens_path,
        headers: api_authorization_headers
      )

      expect(response.body).to eq("ABC123")
    end
  end
end
```

But there are a couple of problems. The way `GitHubToken.generate` works
is that it calls out to the GitHub API, which returns a "random" token. We can't
really write a test for a value that's different every time. Nor would it be desirable
for our test to hit a third-party service, for the reasons we saw in the previous
section. For context, here's what the `GitHubToken` class looks like.

The other problem is that `GitHubToken` hits the GitHub API. Here's what
`GitHubToken` looks like.

```
require "jwt"
require "octokit"

class GitHubToken
  def self.generate(installation_id)
    raise "Installation ID is missing" if installation_id.blank?
    token(installation_id)
  end

  def self.token(installation_id)
    # GITHUB_PRIVATE_PEM comes from the private key which can
    # be generated at
    # https://github.com/settings/apps/saturnci-development
    private_pem = Rails.configuration.github_private_pem
    private_key = OpenSSL::PKey::RSA.new(private_pem)

    payload = {
      iat: Time.now.to_i, # Issued-at time
      exp: Time.now.to_i + (10 * 60), # JWT expiration time
      iss: ENV["GITHUB_APP_ID"]
```

```
    }

    jwt = JWT.encode(payload, private_key, "RS256")
    client = Octokit::Client.new(bearer_token: jwt)

    installation_token = client
      .create_app_installation_access_token(installation_id)

    installation_token[:token]
  end
end
```

So we want to write a test for `GitHubTokensController`. What does that actually mean? What's the behavior we want to target? The behavior we're mainly interested in is not how the token gets generated but in *how the GitHub tokens API endpoint responds to a request for a token.*

With that in mind, we can simply bypass the token generation behavior and insert our own hard-coded value instead. We can do this by *stubbing* the `GitHubToken#generate` method.

```
allow(GitHubToken).to receive(:generate).and_return("ABC123")
```

This line says "when the `generate` method is called on the `GitHubToken` class, don't actually call the method, but instead return the hard-coded value 'ABC123' ". Since we called `allow(GitHubToken).to receive(:generate).and_return("ABC123")` before calling the post method that invokes `GitHubTokensController#create`, the `GitHubToken.generate` method, instead of executing, will simply return "ABC123".

```
require "rails_helper"
include APIAuthenticationHelper

RSpec.describe "GitHub tokens", type: :request do
  describe "POST /api/v1/github_tokens" do
    it "returns a token" do
      allow(GitHubToken).to receive(:generate).and_return("ABC123")

      post(
        api_v1_github_tokens_path,
        headers: api_authorization_headers
      )

      expect(response.body).to eq("ABC123")
    end
  end
end
```

So...we're telling `GitHubToken` to return "ABC123" and then we're asserting that the response body is "ABC123". Is our test pointless?

No, it isn't pointless. We're testing everything that happens *after* the token gets generated, which is definitely more than nothing. We're testing the piece of behavior that takes the return value of
`GitHubToken.generate` and packages it up into an HTTP response. If we were not to have written this test, our application could omit this controller entirely and all our tests would still pass. So, even though it might not look like much, our test serves a valuable purpose indeed.

7.6   Third-party interaction example: data ingestion

This example is actually about how to *avoid* the need for stubbing via loosely-coupled design.

In this example, we want to write a program to keep track of all the people currently in space, plus all the people who have been in space in the past. There's a public API called *People in Space Right Now*, located at
`http://api.open-notify.org/astros.json`, which will show us what people are in space at any given moment. Below is a sample of what a GET request to the API endpoint will return.

```
{
  "people": [
    {
      "craft": "ISS",
      "name": "Sunita Williams"
    },
    {
      "craft": "Tiangong",
      "name": "Li Cong"
    },
    {
      "craft": "Tiangong",
      "name": "Ye Guangfu"
    }
  ],
  "number": 3,
  "message": "success"
}
```

How shall we use this API to achieve our program's objectives? In the spirit of tests as specifications (see chapter 2), let's specify exactly how we want our program to behave.

7.7 People in space tracker specifications

Before we come up with detailed specifications, it may be helpful to think of a rough high-level outline for our program's behavior and how we might build it. Perhaps it could go something like the following:

1. Make a request to the People in Space Right Now API

2. For each person in the list...

   (a) If the craft is new, save it to the database, otherwise do nothing

   (b) If the person is new, save him or her to the database, otherwise do nothing

   (c) Create an "import" record, and associate both the person and the craft with the import

As we've seen in several places in this book, testing choices and design choices are inseparable. In this case, the way we design our program will most certainly have an impact on the design of our tests.

7.7.1 Thinking about design

Below is one possible way we could write our program. As you can see, it's just a single method which takes no arguments.

```
def main
  url = URI('http://api.open-notify.org/astros.json')
  response = Net::HTTP.get(url)
  astronaut_data = JSON.parse(response)['people']

  astronaut_data.each do |entry|
    craft = Craft.find_or_create_by(name: entry['craft'])
    astronaut = Person.find_or_create_by(name: entry['name'])
    Import.create(craft: craft, person: person)
  end
end

main
```

How might we test our `main` method? It would be pretty tough. The method is quite monolithic. There's no easy way to separate the business of fetching the data from the business of ingesting the data.

Below is a way that makes the retrieval of the data and the ingestion of the data a bit more separate.

```
class PeopleInSpaceRightNowAPI
  BASE_URL = "http://api.open-notify.org"

  def get
    url = URI("#{BASE_URL}/astros.json")
    response = Net::HTTP.get(url)
    JSON.parse(response)
  end
end

def ingest_people(people)
  ActiveRecord::Base.transaction do
    people.each do |person|
      craft = Craft.find_or_create_by!(name: person["craft"])
      person = Person.find_or_create_by!(name: person["name"])
      Import.create!(craft:, person:)
    end
  end
end

ingest_people(PeopleInSpaceRightNowAPI.get["people"])
```

In the version above, the (perhaps somewhat disturbingly-named)
ingest_people method doesn't care where the data comes from. As long as the
method is given an array that resembles the array that's returned by the People in
Space API, the method will work just fine. In other words, the ingestion of the data
is *loosely coupled* from the retrieval of the data. This allows the ingestion to easily
be tested in isolation.

In fact, we can take this idea even further and decouple ingesting an *individual*
person from the act of ingesting the *list* of people.

```
def ingest_people(people)
  ActiveRecord::Base.transaction do
    people.each { |person| ingest_person(person) }
  end
end

def ingest_person(person)
  craft = Craft.find_or_create_by!(name: person["craft"])
  person = Person.find_or_create_by!(name: person["name"])
  Import.create!(craft:, person:)
end
```

This design gives us the ability to test in isolation the ingestion of an individual
person. With that in mind, let's now decide on our specifications for ingesting just
one individual person.

7.7.2 Specifications for ingesting a single person

Each specification below deals with a single person.

1. Scenario: person's craft is not currently in the database

    (a) Expectation: a new `Craft` record is created

2. Scenario: person's craft is already in the database

    (a) Expectation: no new `Craft` record is created

3. Scenario: person's name is not currently in the database

    (a) Expectation: a new `Person` record is created

4. Scenario: person's name is currently in the database

    (a) Expectation: a new `Person` record is created

Now that we have our scenarios, let's convert our scenarios into tests.

7.7.3 The tests

Here are tests for both the craft scenarios: first when the craft is not already in the database, and then when the craft already is in the database. Thanks to the loosely-coupled design of our code, the tests don't have to have any stubs.

```
RSpec.describe "ingesting a single person" do
  context "craft is not already in database" do
    let!(:person) do
      {
        "craft": "ISS",
        "name": "Sunita Williams",
      }
    end

    it "creates a new craft record" do
      expect { ingest_person(person) }
        .to change { Craft.count }.by(1)
    end
  end

  context "craft is already in database" do
    let!(:person) do
      {
        "craft": "ISS",
        "name": "Sunita Williams",
      }
```

```
      end

    before { create(:craft, name: "ISS") }

    it "does not create a new craft record" do
      expect { ingest_person(person) }
        .not_to change { Craft.count }
    end
  end
end
```

7.8 Mocks

We saw earlier in this chapter that a mock object is like an undercover boss visiting a restaurant. Mr. Boss looks and behaves just like a real customer, but with the difference that Mr. Boss records what he experiences in the restaurant and reports his recordings later.

7.8.1 Building our own mock object from scratch

In the example below, the "restaurant" we're visiting is a method called `kick_off_big_list_job`. We're not sending in an undercover boss yet. Instead we're sending in a regular customer called `ProcessBigListJob.new`. Notice how the `job` argument defaults to `ProcessBigListJob.new` but can be replaced with anything we like. The menu item the customer is ordering is the `.perform` method.

```
def kick_off_big_list_job(job = ProcessBigListJob.new)
  job.perform
end

class ProcessBigListJob
  def perform
    BigList.process
  end
end
```

Here's what a test might look like. First we create an "undercover boss" called `MockedJob.new`. Remember, the undercover boss looks and behaves almost exactly like a real customer, but unlike a real customer, he carefully records his experiences and reports them later. We then send the undercover boss into the restaurant and, finally, interrogate him.

```
RSpec.describe "kicking off the big list job" do
  it "calls .perform" do
    # MockedJob is an undercover boss
```

```
    job = MockedJob.new

    # We send the undercover boss into the restaurant to order
    # the .perform method
    kick_off_big_list_job(job)

    # Finally, we interrogate the undercover boss
    expect(job.perform_called?).to be true
  end
end
```

How exactly are we giving our undercover boss, MockedJob, the ability to record his experiences and report on them? There are a lot of ways we could have done it but here's one way. We can create a class that can serve as a stand-in for ProcessBigListJob (in other words, a mock object) so that no one knows the difference between the real ProcessBigListJob and the fake MockedJob we've created. Here, together, are ProcessBigListJob and MockedJob.

```
class ProcessBigListJob
  def perform
    BigList.process
  end
end

class MockedJob
  def initialize
    @perform_called = false
  end

  def perform
    BigList.process
    @perform_called = true
  end

  def perform_called?
    @perform_called
  end
end
```

You can see that both methods respond to a message called .perform. The difference is that instead of only invoking BigList.process, MockedJob also sets an instance variable to keep track of whether the .perform method was called.

Below is all the code we've written so far, gathered together. If you like, you can put all this code into a file called, for example, big_list_job_spec.rb and run it using RSpec:

```
$ rspec big_list_job_spec.rb
```

You can demonstrate the validity of the test by commenting out the
`job.perform` line in the `kick_off_big_list_job` method and observing that the
test fails.

```
class BigList
  def self.process
    puts "processing big list"
  end
end

class ProcessBigListJob
  def perform
    BigList.process
  end
end

def kick_off_big_list_job(job = ProcessBigListJob.new)
  job.perform
end

class MockedJob
  def initialize
    @perform_called = false
  end

  def perform
    BigList.process
    @perform_called = true
  end

  def perform_called?
    @perform_called
  end
end

RSpec.describe "kicking off the big list job" do
  it "calls .perform" do
    job = MockedJob.new
    kick_off_big_list_job(job)
    expect(job.perform_called?).to be true
  end
end
```

Now that we've seen how mock objects can work in principle by coding our
own mock object, let's take a look at how it's normally done in RSpec tests.

7.8.2 Mocking using RSpec

We've just seen how we can make an assertion that a certain method was called by creating our own mock object. But if we were to write our own custom mock object every time we needed one, our code would quickly get quite tedious and repetitious.

Let's take another look at our test that uses a custom-written mock object.

```
RSpec.describe "kicking off the big list job" do
  it "calls .perform" do
    job = MockedJob.new
    kick_off_big_list_job(job)
    expect(job.perform_called?).to be true
  end
end
```

For comparison, here's a test that uses RSpec's built-in mocking syntax.

```
RSpec.describe "kicking off the big list job" do
  it "calls .perform" do
    job = ProcessBigListJob.new
    expect(job).to receive(:perform)
    kick_off_big_list_job(job)
  end
end
```

Note the differences. First, we're not creating an instance of `MockedJob`. Instead, we're using the real thing, `ProcessBigListJob`. Second, we're not exercising our code and then making our assertion, we're doing it the other way around. Why is this? It's because, if we were to exercise the code and then make the assertion afterward, RSpec wouldn't have any way to know that we wanted to use a mock object instead of the real object created by `ProcessBigListJob.new`. The `expect(job).to receive(:perform)` line allows RSpec to convert `job` into a mock object so that we're able to track whether `job.perform` was called or not.

Here's the full test code for using an RSpec mock object instead of a custom-written mock object. As with the previous test, you can experiment with this test by commenting out `job.perform` and observing the result. You'll get a failure message saying that there was an expectation that the `.perform` method would be invoked but it wasn't.

```
class BigList
  def self.process
    puts "processing big list"
  end
end
```

```ruby
class ProcessBigListJob
  def perform
    BigList.process
  end
end

def kick_off_big_list_job(job = ProcessBigListJob.new)
  job.perform
end

RSpec.describe "kicking off the big list job" do
  it "calls .perform" do
    job = ProcessBigListJob.new
    expect(job).to receive(:perform)
    kick_off_big_list_job(job)
  end
end
```

When it's expensive, inconvenient or impossible to make assertions about our code's behavior based on state, when can instead use mock objects to make assertions about methods that get called. This allows us to make sensible trade-offs between closely replicating production conditions and writing tests that are economical to maintain.

Chapter 8

Flaky tests

Flaky tests are a fact of life. Every team that has tests has flaky tests. The question for a team is not whether they have flaky tests, but whether they keep the flaky test problem under control or allow it to grow into a major nuisance.

When a team has a flaky test problem, what exactly does that mean? What exactly is the problem? The answer is not as straightforward as it may seem. The problem is actually two problems, one being the cause of the other.

When a boat leaks, the crew has not one problem but two. One problem is the water that's in the boat, causing it to lose buoyancy. This problem can be mitigated by bailing out water, but it won't solve the other problem, which is that there are holes in the boat, allowing more water to leak in.

Below is a table which shows the two layers of the leaky boat problem along with their root causes.

Layer	Symptom	Root Cause
Secondary	Water in the boat	Holes in the boat
Primary	Holes in the boat	Poor design? Aging?

Table 8.1: The two layers of the leaky boat problem

Not only is the water in the boat not the entire problem, it's only the *symptom* of a *secondary* problem. The root cause of the water in the boat, which we now see is just a secondary problem, is the holes in the boat. The holes in the boat are the symptom of the primary problem. What's the root cause of the primary problem? What's causing the holes in the boat?

The holes in the boat could be caused by a number of things. It could be, for example, that the design of the boat is flawed in a way that makes the boat more susceptible to leakage. It could be, for example, that the boat is succumbing to age, and the parts of the boat that once worked well (e.g. the seals in the hull) no longer do.

The specific causes of the holes in the boat aren't the important part of the example. The important thing is to realize that the problem is two-layered, and that the root cause of the holes in the boat will need to be addressed in order to stop water coming into the boat.

A flaky test problem is two-layered as well. The most obvious symptom, the flaky tests themselves, is not the main problem but only the symptom of a secondary problem. Flaky tests are caused by instances of *non-determinism*, a concept we'll see more about shortly. If individual flaky tests are the water in the boat, instances of non-determinism are the holes in the boat.

Layer	Symptom	Root Cause
Secondary	Individual flaky tests	Instances of non-determinism (race conditions, environment corruption, randomness, external dependencies in tests, fragile time dependencies in tests)
Primary	Instances of non-determinism (race conditions, environment corruption, randomness, external dependencies in tests, fragile time dependencies in tests)	Application complexity, poor test design

Table 8.2: The two layers of the flaky test problem

What causes instances of non-determinism—race conditions, environment pollution and so on? The cause can be one of two things. The first possible cause is poorly-written tests. Tests can be written, for example, in such a way that makes them susceptible to race conditions. We'll see more on this soon.

The second possible cause is specific kinds of complexity in the application. For example, race conditions can only occur when an application uses concurrency, and so every instance of concurrency is potentially an opportunity for a race condition to arise. Environment state corruption can only happen when parts of the environment are mutable, and so every instance of mutable environment state potentially creates an opportunity for environment state corruption to occur.

But we're getting ahead of ourselves. What exactly is meant by non-determinism? What exactly is meant by race condition, environment state corruption and so on? And for that matter, what exactly is a flaky test?

8.1 What's a flaky test?

A flaky test is a test that passes sometimes and fails sometimes even when no code has changed. Flaky tests cause test runs to fail illegitimately, causing annoyance, wasted time and a numbness to legitimate failures. All flaky tests are caused by some form of *non-determinism*.

8.2 How non-determinism causes flaky tests

Code that's *deterministic* is code that always gives the same output for a given input. All flaky tests are caused by some form of non-determinism. A test can be non-deterministic if either a) the test code is non-deterministic or b) the application code being tested is non-deterministic, or both. In flaky tests there are exactly five causes of non-determinism.

8.2.1 Race conditions

The train near your house stops every day at 8am. You happen to know that it takes exactly nine minutes to walk from your house to the train station, so you know that if you leave your house at 7:50, you'll arrive at the train station at 7:59, just in time to catch the 8:00 train. That's not much of a buffer but you like to live on the edge. Unfortunately, because your buffer is so small, the slightest snag can spoil your plans. One morning you slip on a banana peel and fall flat on your back. You get up, dust yourself off and resume your walk. But then you step on a carelessly-placed rake and bam! it hits you smack in the nose. When you finally arrive at the station you see that it's 8:02 and you've missed the train. That, my friend, is a race condition.

Race conditions are most likely to arise when the buffer is small. In the train scenario, the buffer was only one minute, a one-minute delay was all it took to cause a problem. (Or, if you were to arrive on time but the train were to depart one minute earlier than normal, that would have caused a problem too.) If the buffer were, say, 30 minutes instead of just one, then a race condition would be very unlikely.

Race conditions are fairly common in system tests (tests that exercise the full application stack including the browser). Let's say for instance there's a test that 1) submits a form and then 2) clicks a link on the subsequent page. The relevant lines of the test might look like this.

```
click_on "Submit"
click_on "Home"
```

In the train scenario, the train operates on a fixed timeline. It shows up at 8:00 and either you're there to get on or you aren't. In this scenario, the test runner operates on a fixed timeline. The test runner submits the form and shortly afterward tries to click the link. Either the link is there at that time or it's not.

How long does the test runner wait between submitting the form and trying to click the link? Very little. Such little time that even if the form response loads quickly, it doesn't always load in time for the link to get clicked by the test runner. The test runner is like a very impation train. It will stop at the station but then it will start moving again immediately after it stops. If you arrive at 7:59 you're good but if you arrive at 8:01 you're out of luck.

How do we fix this race condition? Metaphorically, we have to tell the train conductor to wait. We have to let the conductor know that a very important person is planning to board the train and that the train should not leave without this person.

How do we do that? By adding an `expect(page).to have_content` command immediately after the command that submits the form. Unlike the indifferent `click_on` command, `expect(page).to have_content` will wait a bit before it gives up and allows the test runner to continue.

```
click_on "Submit"
expect(page).to have_content("Thanks") # to prevent race condition
click_on "Home"
```

In the above snippet, the race condition is fixed because the test runner won't proceed past `expect(page).to have_content("Thanks")` until it sees "Thanks" on the page. By proxy we know we're on the same page that contains the "Home" link.

8.2.2 Environment state corruption

Tests can create flaky behavior when they spoil the environment in which they run.

Let's use another analogy to illustrate this one. Let's say I wanted to perform two tests on myself. The first test is to see if I can shoot an apple off the top of my friend's head with a bow and arrow. The second test is to see if I can drink 10 shots of tequila in under an hour.

If I were to perform the arrow test immediately followed by the tequila test repeatedly, I could expect to get basically the same test results each time, provided I allowed myself enough time to sober up between tests.

But if I were to perform the tequila test immediately followed by the arrow test, my aim would probably be compromised, and I might miss the apple once in a while. The problem is that the tequila test spoils its environment: it creates a lasting alteration in the global state, and that alteration affects subsequent tests.

If I were to perform these two tests in random order, the tequila test would give the same result each time because I'd always be starting it sober, but the arrow test would appear to "flake" because sometimes I'd start it sober and sometimes I'd start it drunk. I might even suspect that there's a problem with the arrow test because that's the test that's showing the symptom. But I'd be wrong. The problem is a different test that spoils the environment.

There are a number of ways a test can alter its environment and create non-deterministic behavior.

One way is to alter database data. Imagine two tests, each of which creates a user with the email address `test@example.com`. The first test will pass and, if there's a unique constraint on `users.email`, the second test will raise an error due to the unique constraint violation. Sometimes the first test will fail and sometimes the second test will fail, depending on the order in which order you run them.

Another way that a test could spoil its environment is to change a configuration setting. Let's say that your test environment has background jobs configured not to run for most tests because most background jobs are irrelevant to what's being tested and would just slow things down. But then let's imagine that you have one test where you do want background jobs to run, and so at the beginning of that tests you set background job setting from "don't run" to "run". If you don't remember to change the setting back to "don't run" at the end, background jobs will run for all later tests and potentially cause problematic behavior.

The environment can also be spoiled by changing environment variables, altering the contents of the filesystem, or in any way that causes a lasting change to the test environment.

8.2.3 External dependencies in tests

The main reason why network dependency can create non-deterministic behavior is for the simple reason that sometimes the network is up and sometimes it's not.

Moreover, when you're depending on the network, you're often depending on some third-party service. Even if the network itself is working just fine, the third-party service could suffer an outage at any time, causing your tests to fail. I've also seen cases where a test fails because a test makes a third-party service call over and over and then gets rate-limited, and from that point on, for a period of time, that test fails.

The way to prevent flaky tests caused by network dependence is to stub services rather than hitting live services. See chapter 9 for more details.

8.2.4 Randomness

Randomness is, by definition, non-deterministic. If you have, for example, a test that generates a random integer between 1 and 2 and then asserts that that number is 1, that test is going to fail about half the time. Random inputs lead to random failures.

8.2.5   Fragile time dependencies in tests

Once I was working late and I noticed that some certain tests started to fail for no apparent reason, even though I hadn't changed any code.

After some investigation I realized that, due to the way they were written, these tests would always fail when run at a certain time of day. It just happened that I had just never worked that late before.

This sort of failure is common with tests that cross the boundary of a day (or month or year). Let's say you have a test that creates an appointment that occurs four hours from the current time, and then asserts that that appointment is included on a list of appointments for the current day. That test will pass when it's run at 8am because the appointment will appear at 12pm which is the same day. But the test will fail when it's run at 10pm because four hours after 10pm is 2am which is the next day. The way around this problem is to always use absolute times in tests instead of relative ones.

8.3   How complexity causes non-determinism, and what to do about it

How exactly does application complexity cause non-determinism? First, imagine the other end of the spectrum: a program that's not especially complex, but extremely simple. Perhaps this program is a single tiny Ruby script that does nothing more that print the word "hello" to stdout. The tests for such a program could never flake. The program uses no database, no JavaScript, no libraries, no network, just a single one-line script. The tests for the program could never flake because the program allows no opportunities for non-determinism to arise. There's no concurrency, so there can be no race conditions. There's no mutable environment state, so there can be no environment corruption. There are no external dependencies, so there can be no non-deterministic dependency availability. There's no randomness. There's nothing in the program that involves time, so there can be no non-determinism arising from fragile time dependencies.

Now imagine a program that has all the irreducible complexity that comes along with a normal web application, plus, just for fun, a gratuitous helping of unnecessary complexity as well. Thanks to the fact that this application uses a fancy frontend JavaScript framework and a lot of XHR calls, there are lots of opportunities for race conditions. This application uses dozens of third-party libraries, each with several configuration settings, creating many opportunities for environment corruption to take place. You get the idea. The more complex the application's architecture is, the more opportunities there will be for non-determinism, and therefore the more opportunities there will be for flaky tests.

Problem	Prerequisite
Race conditions	Concurrency
Environment state corruption	Mutable environment state
Randomness	Randomness
External dependencies in tests	External dependencies
Fragile time dependencies	Features that involve time

Table 8.3: Causes of non-determinism and their prerequisites

To summarize all this in a few words, **complicated applications tend to have more flaky tests than simple ones**. The takeaway, of course, is to avoid making your applications any more complicated than they have to be. This might seem like a moot point since it's obviously never desirable to make anything more complicated than it has to be, and no one ever makes a conscious choice to make a program needlessly complex. Yet, needless complexity is everywhere. In fact, in my experience, overcomplexity in web applications is not the exception but the norm.

Part of the reason for this, I believe, is that needless complexity often sneaks into a codebase in disguise. Needless complexity can arise, for example, by simply allowing the program to have too many features and do too much stuff. Engineers can't always influence the scope of the product they're working on, but that doesn't mean that product choices aren't the root cause of certain engineering problems, like flaky tests. Often, the expensive luxury of a feature-rich product and a flashy UI is paid for partly in the form of flaky tests.

Needless complexity can also arise from not realizing the costs of certain architectural choices. A React-Rails app, for example, is more complicated and more expensive than a plain Rails app. Quite often, the supposed benefit is not nearly worth the price paid. Developers often add gems to apps quite cavalierly, not realizing that gems add performance overhead, upgrade costs, security liabilities, and potentially mutable environment state which can lead to flaky tests. Beware of complexity. It's often very easy to add and extremely difficult to take away.

8.4 Why tests flake more on CI than locally

You may have found, to your frustration, that tests that flake on CI rarely misbehave when run locally. Why is this?

Remember that one of the causes of flaky tests is when one test spoils its environment and interferes with later tests. If a test is flaking for this reason and it's run by itself, it won't flake, since the only way to get it to flake would be to run the environment-spoiling test before it.

Another reason is that on CI, flaky test conditions simply have more opportunities to arise than in a local environment. If a certain test fails one in 1000 times, then you'll surely see it fail on CI once in a while because the CI service is running the entire test suite multiple times per day. But when you run the same test locally, it's improbable that you'll get to see the test fail without running it a large number of times.

Lastly, differences in resource configuration (memory, processor speed, etc.) between your local machines and the CI environment can cause differences in how likely tests are to flake. Remember that race conditions occur when two concurrent processes need to complete in a certain order but sometimes they finish in the wrong order. In your local environment, process A may complete well before process B and so there's no race condition. In a CI environment, process B might take longer and occasionally finish after process A, causing a race condition and an occasional failure.

The fact that tests flake more in a CI environment than locally can make flaky tests devilishly hard to diagnose and fix. Let's take a look at some ways to approach this process.

8.5   How to fix flaky tests

Flaky tests are hard to fix largely because they're hard to reproduce. If a flaky test can't be consistently reproduced then it's very hard to hypothesize about the conditions that make it fail.

It's also hard to hypothesize about the cause of a flaky test if we don't have enough background knowledge to guide our hypotheses. If we're familiar with the conditions that can lead to flaky tests then we can come up with much more intelligent guesses than if we're clueless about how flaky tests arise.

The fact that flaky tests are hard to reproduce also means that our fix attempts are hard to validate or invalidate. We could apply a fix and then not know if it actually worked until days or weeks later, since that's how long it might take for the test to flake again.

Given these difficulties, how do we fix flaky tests?

8.5.1   Adopt an effective bugfix methodology

Fixing a bug is easier, faster and more pleasant when we approach it methodically instead of haphazardly. This is especially true when fixing flaky tests because flaky tests tend to be trickier to fix than other types of bugs.

I find it helpful to split the bugfix process into three distinct stages: reproduction, diagnosis and fix. When fixing a bug, it's very easy to let your head get filled with a jumble of thoughts and lose track of what you're doing. Dividing the process into steps helps us stay focused on one activity at a time.

In the sections that follow we'll see how the reproduce-diagnose-fix process applies to fixing flaky tests.

8.5.2   Arm yourself with background knowledge

All bug diagnoses start as guesses. The only way to diagnose a bug is to make a guess and then perform some tests to see if the guess is right. Not all guesses are equally good of course. The narrower the scope of possibilities, the more efficient the guess-and-check process will be. For example, if a doctor sees a patient who is coughing, the doctor will probably narrow the scope of her initial guesses to respiratory issues, since she has the background knowledge that tells her that these two things are related. Similarly, a familiarity with the causes of flaky tests will allow you to narrow your hypotheses to the most likely ones instead of making wild guesses. To get more efficient in diagnosing flaky tests, commit the five causes of flaky tests to memory.

8.5.3   Before reproducing: determine whether it's really a flaky test

Not everything that appears to be a flaky test is actually a flaky test. Sometimes a test that appears to be flaking is just a healthy test that's legitimately failing.

So when I see a test that's supposedly flaky, I like to try to find multiple instances of that test flaking before I accept its flakiness as a fact. And even then, there's no law that says that a test that previously flaked can't fail legitimately at some point in the future. So the first step is to make sure that the problem I'm solving really is the problem I think I'm solving.

8.5.4   Reproducing a flaky test

My go-to method for reproducing a flaky test is simply to re-run the test suite multiple times on my CI service until I see the flaky test fail. I like to run the test suite a large number of times to not only reproduce the failure but also to get a feel for how frequently the flaky test fails. The actions I take during the bugfix process may be different depending on how frequently the test fails, as we'll see later on.

Sometimes a flaky test fails so infrequently that it's practically impossible to get the test to fail on demand. When this happens, it's impossible to tell whether the test is passing due to random chance or because the flakiness has legitimately gone away. The way I handle these cases is to deprioritize the fix attempt and wait for the test to fail again in the natural course of business. This way I can be sure that I'm not wasting my time trying to fix a problem that's not really there.

Now let's turn to diagnosis.

8.5.5   Diagnosing a flaky test

When trying to diagnose a flaky test, it can often feel like you have nothing to go off of and no way to make progress. Here are some actions you can take that will help you move forward with the diagnosis process no matter what.

Read the failure message, the test code and the application code. Obviously, the very least you can do is lay eyes on the test failure message and the code that's related to it. As you look at the code, ask yourself, do you fully understand all of it? If not, what can you do to gain a better understanding? Remember that if you perfectly understood all the code and the tests, you would also understand the cause of the flaky test you're trying to diagnose. All that lies between you and a diagnosis is a certain amount of understanding. Even though you'll of course never understand all of the code and all of the tests in a non-trivial software system, you can begin working in that direction. Eventually you'll have enough understanding to arrive at a diagnosis.

Make the test code and application code as easy to understand as possible. Chances are that the current test code and application code aren't as easy to understand as they possibly could be. If they were, then the cause of the flaky test would probably be easier to identify. Any place where the test code or application code are harder to understand than they could be is an unnecessary obstacle to diagnosing the flaky test. If you fix these weaknesses then your diagnosis work will be easier.

Make the test environment as easy to understand as possible. Sometimes a crappy test environment adds friction and annoyance to the diagnosis process. For example, maybe the test suite contains too much background data, which makes it hard to understand what's in the database at any given time.

Check the tests that ran just before the flaky test. The idea with this tactic is to see if the tests that ran before the flaky test may have altered the test environment in a way that causes a flaky test.

Add diagnostic info to the test. A test failure doesn't always give you as much helpful information as you would wish. Sometimes it's possible to add some debug output to the test and/or the application code so you can get a clearer picture of what's going on.

Perform a binary search. Remember that all bug diagnoses start out as guesses, and the narrower the scope of the guess, the more likely the guess is to be right. A *binary search* is a way of efficiently tarrowing down the scope of the guess by repeatedly dividing the scope in half. A full description of binary search is outside the scope of this book, but good articles on the topic can be readily found online.

Repeat all the above steps. If you carry out all these steps and then start over from the beginning, you might see things with a little bit more perspective. Beware of giving up on the flaky test too early and without justification. It's common for developers to spend some time trying to fix a flaky test, decide it's a mystery and then move onto something else without having fixed anything.

8.5.6 Applying the fix for a flaky test

Once you've spent some time trying to diagnose the flaky test, hopefully you'll have a hypothesis that seems strong enough to be worth testing. The next step with a normal bugfix would be to apply the fix and then carry out the reproduction steps to see if the fix actually worked. Since flaky tests can be so hard to reproduce on demand, this step sometimes must be handled differently for flaky tests. Sometimes the only way to see if a flaky test fix attempt worked is to wait. If the test in question only fails at a rate of about once a month, you'll have to wait several months after the fix is applied to declare victory.

8.5.7 Don't delete a test without a good reason

There are two benefits to fixing a flaky test. One benefit of course is that the test will no longer flake. The other is that you gain some skill in fixing flaky tests as well as a better understanding of what causes flaky tests. This means that fixing flaky tests creates a positive feedback loop. The more flaky tests you fix, the more quickly and easily you can fix future flaky tests, and the fewer flaky tests you'll write in the first place because you'll know what mistakes not to make.

If you simply delete a flaky test, you're depriving yourself of those benefits. And of course, you're also destroying whatever value that test had. It's usually better to push through and keep working on fixing the flaky test until the job is done.

It might sometimes seem like the amount of time it takes to fix a certain flaky test is more than the value of that test can justify. Remember that the important thing is not the cost/benefit ratio of any individual flaky test fix, but the cost/benefit ratio of all the flaky test fixes on average. Sometimes flaky test fixes will take 20 minutes and sometimes they'll take two weeks. The flaky test fixes that take two weeks might feel unjustifiable, but if you have a general policy of just giving up when things get too hard and deleting the test, then your test-fixing skills will always stay limited, and your weak skills will incur a cost on the test suite for as long as you keep deleting difficult flaky tests. Better to just bite the bullet and develop the skills to fix hard flaky test cases.

Having said all that, deleting a flaky test is sometimes, in rare cases, the right move. As we saw in chapter 4, some types of tests are pointless. When a flaky test coincidentally happens to also be pointless, it's better to just delete the test than to pay the cost to fix a test that doesn't have any value.

Skipping flaky tests is similar in spirit to deleting them. Skipping a flaky test has all the same downsides as deleting it, plus now you have the extra overhead of occasionally stumbling across the test and remembering "Oh yeah, I should fix this eventually." And what's worse, the skipped test often gets harder to fix as time goes on because the skipped test is frozen in time but the rest of the codebase continues to change in ways that aren't compatible with tests. The easiest time to fix a flaky test is right when the flakiness is first discovered.

Chapter 9

Testing sins and crimes

The name of this chapter is of course tongue-in-cheek. Some of the practices here aren't exactly *wrong*, they're just costly, and only make sense in exceptional circumstances when the alternative would be even worse.

9.1 Writing tests as verifications, not specifications

Remember that the aim of testing is not to ask "did it work?" bet rather "did it work as specified?"

The test below was written under a verification mindset, not a specification mindset. The clues to this fact are a) that the test description says that it *"correctly transfers the balance"* (without specifying what "correctly" means) and b) that the body of the test contains assertion after assertion, "making sure it worked".

```
RSpec.describe BankAccount, type: :model do
  let(:sender) { FactoryBot.create(:bank_account, balance: 1000) }
  let(:receiver) { FactoryBot.create(:bank_account, balance: 500) }
  let(:transfer_amount) { 200 }

  describe "balance transfer" do
    before do
      sender.transfer_to(receiver, transfer_amount)
      sender.reload
      receiver.reload
    end

    it "correctly transfers the balance" do
      total_balance = sender.balance + receiver.balance
      expect(sender.balance).to eq(800)
      expect(receiver.balance).to eq(700)
      expect(total_balance).to eq(1500)
      expect(sender.transactions.last.amount).to eq(-transfer_amount)
```

```
      expect(receiver.transactions.last.amount).to eq(transfer_amount)
      expect(sender.balance).to be >= 0
      expect(sender.last_transaction_status).to eq('completed')
      expect(receiver.last_transaction_status).to eq('completed')
    end
  end
end
```

Converting the `describe` and `it` blocks above to bullet point items, here's how the test above could read:

- Balance transfer

    – It correctly transfers the balance

This description of the test doesn't convey much meaning since it doesn't specify what "correctly" means. Here's a different, more meaningful way to express the test.

- When the source account has sufficient funds

    – It decreases the sender's balance by the transfer amount

    – It increases the receiver's balance by the transfer amount

- When the source account does not have sufficient funds

    – It does not change the sender's balance

    – It does not change the receiver's balance

If we convert the primary bullet points to `context` blocks and the secondary bullet points to `it` blocks, the test could look like this.

```
RSpec.describe BankAccount, type: :model do
  context "when the source account has sufficient funds" do
    let(:sender) { FactoryBot.create(:bank_account, balance: 1000) }
    let(:receiver) { FactoryBot.create(:bank_account, balance: 500) }

    it "decreases the sender's balance by the transfer amount" do
      sender.transfer_to(receiver, 200)
      expect(sender.reload.balance).to eq(800)
    end

    it "increases the receiver's balance by the transfer amount" do
      sender.transfer_to(receiver, 200)
      expect(receiver.reload.balance).to eq(700)
    end
  end
```

```
context "when the source account does not have sufficient funds" do
  let(:sender) { FactoryBot.create(:bank_account, balance: 150) }
  let(:receiver) { FactoryBot.create(:bank_account, balance: 500) }

  it "does not change the sender's balance" do
    sender.transfer_to(receiver, 200)
    expect(sender.balance).to eq(150)
  end

  it "does not change the receiver's balance" do
    sender.transfer_to(receiver, 200)
    expect(receiver.balance).to eq(500)
  end
end
end
```

This test is both meaningful and easier to understand because it focuses on specifying behavior, not verifying that the behavior occurred.

9.2 Testing implementation rather than behavior

As we saw in chapter 4 on writing meaningful tests, tests are meaningful when they test *ends*, not just means to ends. Tests are meaningful when they test behavior, not implementation. The tests below are not very meaningful because they focus exclusively on implementation.

```
it { is_expected.to have_many(:comments).dependent(:nullify) }
it { is_expected.to have_many(:feed_events).dependent(:delete_all) }
it { is_expected.to have_many(:mentions).dependent(:delete_all) }
it { is_expected.to have_many(:notifications).dependent(:delete_all) }
it { is_expected.to have_many(:page_views).dependent(:delete_all) }
```

These tests lack meaning and usefulness. They essentially just ask: is the code I wrote the code I wrote? They're just a direct restatement of the code itself.

Sometimes, in rare cases, usually in legacy projects with nasty code dependencies, tests that focus on means are the best that can be done, since there's no good way to write a test for the end that the means supports. In these scenarios the value of an "implementation test" is more than zero, since the alternative is no test at all. Just keep in mind the difference between making an exception for specific reasons and writing implementation tests as a general policy.

9.3 Modifying production code for the sake of tests

If I add a conditional to my code to make it behave differently in the test environment than in the development or production environment, then I'm not really testing my real code. Furthermore, environment sniffing (e.g. `Rails.env.test?`) adds distracting and confusing noise that makes the code harder to understand.

9.4   Overgeneralization

In general, specific examples are easier to understand than vague ones. By definition, the more general a term is, the more different things it could mean. The assertion below uses two terms, `subject` and `expected_result`, both of which could mean literally anything.

```
expect(subject).to eq(expected_result)
```

Better to use specific values. Don't be afraid to hard-code expected values, even if it means repeating them.

```
expect(user.last_name).to eq("Kowalski")
```

Remember: duplication means duplicated *behavior*. Tests aren't behavior, they're specifications. Duplicating test code rarely comes with the same costs and risks that duplicating application code does. Clarity beats conciseness.

9.5   Misapplying DRY

As we saw in chapter 6 on duplication, the DRY principle applies differently to test code than application code. If I'm hesitant to allow duplication in my test code, then I might end up with parts of tests that look something like this:

```
expect(subject[0]["#{expected_result[0].keys[0]}_"]).to eq(1)
```

In this test, I've used `subject` so that I don't have to repeat whatever the test subject is and I've defined an `expected_result` array so I don't have to repeat what the expected result is. But, awkwardly, I only need part of `expected_result` for this test and so I have to dig deeply into `expected_result` to get the relevant part.

What might be the meaning of this test? Who knows. My misdirected attempt to keep my test code DRY has completely obscured the test's meaning.

9.6   Turning tests into mini-programs

Some tests are so complicated that they're basically programs unto themselves. The example below is very hard to follow.

```ruby
context "when a target_article_id is provided" do
  it "favors records containing the target_article_id" do
    allow(FeatureFlag).to receive(:enabled?)
      .with(:article_id_adjusted_weight)
      .and_return(true)

    described_class.delete_all
    target_article_id = 123
    favored_weight_multiplier = 10

    # Create billboards with different weights and article_ids
    bb1 = create(
      :billboard,
      weight: 5,
      preferred_article_ids: [target_article_id]
    )

    bb2 = create(:billboard, weight: 1, preferred_article_ids: [])

    bb3 = create(
      :billboard,
      weight: 1,
      preferred_article_ids: [target_article_id]
    )

    bb4 = create(:billboard, weight: 2, preferred_article_ids: [])
    bb5 = create(:billboard, weight: 1, preferred_article_ids: [])

    # Adjusted total weight accounting for the favored records
    total_weight = (5 * favored_weight_multiplier)
      + 1 + (1 * favored_weight_multiplier) + 2 + 1

    expected_probabilities = {
      bb1.id => (5.0 * favored_weight_multiplier) / total_weight,
      bb2.id => 1.0 / total_weight,
      bb3.id => (1.0 * favored_weight_multiplier) / total_weight,
      bb4.id => 2.0 / total_weight,
      bb5.id => 1.0 / total_weight
    }

    counts = Hash.new(0)
    num_trials = 5_000

    num_trials.times do
      id = described_class.weighted_random_selection(
        described_class.all,
        target_article_id
      ).id
```

```
        counts[id] += 1
    end

    counts.each do |id, count|
      observed_probability = count.to_f / num_trials
      expected_probability = expected_probabilities[id]

      expect(observed_probability)
        .to be_within(0.025).of(expected_probability)
    end
  end
end
```

When a test is "static", with hard-coded values and no moving parts, it's easier to understand because there's less changing state to follow and the execution path is simpler. When the test is a whole program itself, like the one above, the test is much harder to interpret.

9.7   Unclear names

It's easy, in tests, to get lazy and give entities names like `note1` and `note2` in the example below. Sometimes names like this are appropriate because there truly is no meaningful distinction between the two items. But most of the time, the entities in tests do have meaning, and the test can be more easily understood if the entities in the test are given names that match their meaning.

```
RSpec.describe AccountModerationNote do
  describe 'chronological scope' do
    it 'returns account moderation notes oldest to newest' do
      account = Fabricate(:account)

      note1 = Fabricate(
        :account_moderation_note,
        target_account: account
      )

      note2 = Fabricate(
        :account_moderation_note,
        target_account: account
      )

      expect(account.targeted_moderation_notes.chronological)
        .to eq [note1, note2]
    end
  end
end
```

The names `note1` and `note2` are meaningless. It would make the test easier to understand if instead we name the two notes, say, `newer_note` and `older_note`.

```
RSpec.describe AccountModerationNote do
  describe 'chronological scope' do
    it 'returns account moderation notes oldest to newest' do
      account = Fabricate(:account)
      newer_note = Fabricate(
        :account_moderation_note,
        target_account: account
      )

      older_note = Fabricate(
        :account_moderation_note,
        target_account: account
      )

      expect(account.targeted_moderation_notes.chronological)
        .to eq [older_note, newer_note]
    end
  end
end
```

Now, in the assertion, we can clearly see that the older note appears in the list before the newer note. This agrees with the test description of "it returns account moderation notes oldest to newest". It's a simple but surprisingly seldom-followed rule of thumb: call things what they are!

9.8 Conglomerated setup data

It's rare that every single test case in a file has the same setup data needs. Many times, several test cases require a slight variation on the data that the other tests need. How do we address these varied setup data needs?

Sadly, one of the most common ways to address this need is to create a single body of data that can cover every possible scenario. What's bad about this? The more complicated the setup data, the higher a cognitive toll it incurs. When setup data from multiple tests gets merged, the cognitive toll is increased, often not just additively but multiplicatively.

Take a look at the following test case. The values it needs include `old_status`, `very_old_status` and `slightly_less_old_status`.

```
it 'returns statuses included the max_id and older than the' \
   'max_id but not newer than max_id' do
  expect(subject)
    .to include(old_status.id)
```

```
    .and include(very_old_status.id)
    .and not_include(slightly_less_old_status.id)
end
```

Now take a look at the setup code that precedes this test. Buckle up, it's a long ride.

```
describe '#statuses_to_delete' do
  subject { account_statuses_cleanup_policy.statuses_to_delete }

  let!(:unrelated_status) { Fabricate(:status, created_at: 3.years.ago) }

  let!(:very_old_status) do
    Fabricate(:status, created_at: 3.years.ago, account: account)
  end

  let!(:pinned_status) do
    Fabricate(:status, created_at: 1.year.ago, account: account)
  end

  let!(:direct_message) do
    Fabricate(
      :status,
      created_at: 1.year.ago,
      account: account,
      visibility: :direct
    )
  end

  let!(:self_faved) do
    Fabricate(:status, created_at: 1.year.ago, account: account)
  end

  let!(:self_bookmarked) do
    Fabricate(:status, created_at: 1.year.ago, account: account)
  end

  let!(:status_with_poll) do
    Fabricate(
      :status,
      created_at: 1.year.ago,
      account: account,
      poll_attributes: {
        account: account,
        voters_count: 0,
        options: %w(a b),
        expires_in: 2.days
      }
```

```
    )
  end

  let!(:status_with_media) do
    Fabricate(:status, created_at: 1.year.ago, account: account)
  end

  let!(:faved_primary) do
    Fabricate(:status, created_at: 1.year.ago, account: account)
  end

  let!(:faved_secondary) do
    Fabricate(:status, created_at: 1.year.ago, account: account)
  end

  let!(:reblogged_primary) do
    Fabricate(:status, created_at: 1.year.ago, account: account)
  end

  let!(:reblogged_secondary) do
    Fabricate(:status, created_at: 1.year.ago, account: account)
  end

  let!(:recent_status) do
    Fabricate(:status, created_at: 2.days.ago, account: account)
  end

  before do
    Fabricate(
      :media_attachment,
      account: account,
      status: status_with_media
    )

    Fabricate(:status_pin, account: account, status: pinned_status)
    Fabricate(:favourite, account: account, status: self_faved)
    Fabricate(:bookmark, account: account, status: self_bookmarked)

    faved_primary.status_stat.update(favourites_count: 4)
    faved_secondary.status_stat.update(favourites_count: 5)
    reblogged_primary.status_stat.update(reblogs_count: 4)
    reblogged_secondary.status_stat.update(reblogs_count: 5)
  end

  context 'when passed a max_id' do
    subject do
      account_statuses_cleanup_policy
        .statuses_to_delete(50, old_status.id)
```

```
      .pluck(:id)
  end

  let!(:old_status) do
    Fabricate(:status, created_at: 1.year.ago, account: account)
  end

  let!(:slightly_less_old_status) do
    Fabricate(:status, created_at: 6.months.ago, account: account)
  end

  it 'returns statuses included the max_id and older than the' \
     'max_id but not newer than max_id' do
    expect(subject)
      .to include(old_status.id)
      .and include(very_old_status.id)
      .and not_include(slightly_less_old_status.id)
  end
 end
end
```

Of all the setup code that comes before this test, what's needed and what's not?
Maybe it's all needed. More likely, only a little bit of it is needed. There's no easy
way to know.

9.9   Superfluous assertions or setup data

Tests are easiest to understand when they're only as complicated as they need to be
and no more. Study the test below and work out what it's doing as best you can.

```
RSpec.describe "Display users search spec", js: true do
  let(:current_user) do
    create(:user, username: "ironman", name: "Iron Man")
  end

  let(:found_user) do
    create(:user, username: "janedoe", name: "Jane Doe")
  end

  let(:found_two_user)
    create(:user, username: "doejane", name: "Doe Jane")
  end

  let(:not_found_user)
    create(:user, username: "batman", name: "Batman")
  end
```

```
  it "returns correct results for name search" do
    current_user
    found_user
    found_two_user
    not_found_user
    visit "/search?q=jane&filters=class_name:User"

    expect(page).to have_content(found_user.name)
    expect(page).to have_content(found_two_user.name)
    expect(page).not_to have_content(current_user.name)
    expect(page).not_to have_content(not_found_user.name)
  end
end
```

Seeing current_user, found_user, found_two_user and not_found_user makes me wonder what the significance of each of these users is and how they're different. But it turns out there's not much difference. In fact, we can do everything we need to do in this test using just *one* user!

```
RSpec.describe "Display users search spec", js: true do
  before do
    create(:user, username: "janedoe", name: "Jane Doe")
  end

  context "search query matches first name" do
    it "finds the user" do
      visit "/search?q=jane&filters=class_name:User"
      expect(page).to have_content("janedoe")
    end
  end

  context "search query does not match first name" do
    it "does not find the user" do
      visit "/search?q=blah&filters=class_name:User"
      expect(page).to have_content("janedoe")
    end
  end
end
```

Including multiple redundant examples that do the same thing usually doesn't serve to make the test clearer. Usually it just makes the meaning more obscure.

9.10   Skipping or deleting flaky tests

As we saw in chapter 9 on flaky tests, skipping or deleting flaky tests hurts you twice. First, you lose the value of the test that's being deleted. Second, you miss out on building your flaky-test-fixing skills.

There's just one scenario where it's smart to delete a flaky test: when a test is both flaking and happens, by coincidence, to have no value either.

9.11   Invalid assertions

It's surprisingly easy to write a test that gives a false positive, false negative or in some other way fails to enforce the target behavior.

The test below will fail. But not because the feature is now working! It will fail because the test is invalid.

```
RSpec.describe "test reports", type: :request do
  describe "POST /api/v1/jobs/:id/test_reports" do
    let!(:job) { create(:job) }

    it "adds a report to a job" do
      post(
        api_v1_job_test_reports_path(job_id: job.id),
        params: "test report content",
        headers: api_authorization_headers.merge(
          { "CONTENT_TYPE" => "text/plain" }
        )
      )

      expect(job.test_report).to eq("test report content")
    end
  end
end
```

The reason the test will erroneously fail is because the `job` record is stale. The value we sent to the API endpoint did in fact get saved to the database, but in order to have access to that value, we need to call `job.reload` in order to load the most recent database value into memory.

```
expect(job.reload.test_report).to eq("test report content")
```

This is why it's a good idea not just to write tests but to perform tests to verify the validity of our tests. If that sounds recursive, don't worry. It doesn't go any layers deeper than that.

9.12   Using send

Sometimes in tests you may see Ruby's `send` method being used in order to invoke private methods without raising an error. This defeats the purpose of private methods, which is to hide methods from an object's public API so that they may be refactored freely.

When I see `send` being used in a test, I usually just make the method public so `send` doesn't have to be used anymore. This of course destroys any benefit there may have been to the method having been private, but usually I find the trade-off to be worth it.

9.13 Using sleep

We saw in chapter 9 that many flaky tests are caused by race conditions. Race conditions can often be fixed by simply adding a `sleep` to the test. This way, in the race between the test runner and the system under test, the test runner will be less likely to "win" the race and cause a problem. Unfortunately, this "solution" really only fixes the symptom of the problem, not the root cause, and it makes tests slower than they need to be. A better solution is just to find out what the actual root cause of the race condition is and fix that.

9.14 Inverted let dependency

In the following test, we can see that 1) a `user` gets created and then, later on, 2) a `client_app` gets created. Right?

Actually, no! When RSpec's `let` helper is given a block, the block doesn't get invoked immediately. Instead, `let` creates a memoized method (see chapter 13 for details) which doesn't get invoked until the first time the value is referenced.

In the case of `let(:user)`, the first time `user` is referenced is in the first line of the `it 'logs in'` spec. When `user.confirmation_token` is called, it causes the `user` method to be called (remember, `let(:user)` will define a memoized method called `user`) which will invoke the body of the block associated with the `let` statement.

Then, because the user's `created_by_application` attribute depends on `client_app`, the `client_app` method defined by the later `let(:client_app)` statement will be invoked. So even though `client_app` is nested more deeply than `user` and appears after `user`, it's `user` that depends on `client_app`, not the other way around.

```
RSpec.describe 'email confirmation flow when captcha is enabled' do
  let(:user) do
    Fabricate(
      :user,
      confirmed_at: nil,
      confirmation_token: 'foobar',
      created_by_application: client_app
    )
  end
```

```
before do
  allow(Auth::ConfirmationsController)
    .to receive(:new).and_return(stubbed_controller)
end

context 'when the user signed up through an app' do
  let(:client_app) { Fabricate(:application) }

  it 'logs in' do
    visit "/auth/confirmation?confirmation_token=" \
      "#{user.confirmation_token}&redirect_to_app=true"

    # It presents the user with a captcha form
    expect(page).to have_title(
      I18n.t('auth.captcha_confirmation.title')
    )

    # It redirects to app and confirms user
    expect { click_on I18n.t('challenge.confirm') }
      .to change { user.reload.confirmed? }.from(false).to(true)

    expect(page).to have_current_path(
      /\A#{client_app.confirmation_redirect_uri}/,
      url: true
    )
  end
end
end
```

Dear reader, it is madness. Instead of this confusing inverted `let` dependency, I suggest something more like the following.

```
RSpec.describe 'email confirmation flow when captcha is enabled' do
  let!(:client_app) { Fabricate(:application) }

  let!(:user) do
    Fabricate(
      :user,
      confirmed_at: nil,
      confirmation_token: 'foobar',
      created_by_application: client_app
    )
  end
```

Since user depends on `client_app`, the new version of the test puts `client_app` first. We lay the base before we put things on top of it.

Additionally, changing each `let` to `let!` makes it so the memoized methods created by `let` get invoked immediately instead of waiting for them to appear somewhere in the test. This makes the execution path easier to follow.

9.15   Tautological tests

A *tautology* is a statement that is true in every possible interpretation. For example, the statement "all humans are people" is a tautology. Under the ordinary definitions of "humans" and "people", there's no condition under which the statement could be false.

Below is a test whose assertion can never be false.

```
RSpec.describe BankService do
  describe '#get_account_balance' do
    let(:account_id) { '12345' }

    before do
      allow_any_instance_of(BankApiClient)
        .to receive(:fetch_account_balance)
        .with(account_id)
        .and_return({ success: true, balance: 5000 })
    end

    it 'returns the exact balance that was stubbed' do
      response = BankApiClient.fetch_account_balance(account_id)
      expect(response).to eq({ success: true, balance: 5000 })
    end
  end
end
```

The test is tautological because it merely tests the value that it just stubbed. Here's what the test is doing:

1. Stub `fetch_account_balance` to return 5000

2. Call `fetch_account_balance`

3. Assert that the result was 5000

If we stub a method to return a certain value and then call the method, it will of course always returned the value we told it to return. Such a test doesn't test the behavior of the method, it completely bypasses it. There's no scenario in which tautological tests are worth writing; they're simply illogical.

Part II

Tools

Chapter 10

Ruby DSLs

RSpec, Factory Bot and Capybara—all of which are very widely used tools in Rails testing—all make heavy use of domain-specific languages (DSLs). In order to deeply understand these tools one needs to understand Ruby DSLs.

10.1 Messages

In Ruby, we don't call methods on objects. Rather, we *send messages* to objects. The object receives the message and decides what to do with it. Maybe the object will decide to use the message to invoke a method. Maybe it will do something else. It's a subtle distinction, and usually we can ignore it, but the principle of sending messages rather than calling methods will be important as we get deeper into this chapter.

10.2 Blocks

A block is a way of passing *behavior* rather than *data* to a method. To easy gently into blockland, we'll first look at some native Ruby methods that make use of blocks. Then we'll see how to write our own custom methods that use blocks.

10.2.1 Native Ruby methods that take blocks

Here are four native Ruby methods that take blocks. For each one, I'll give a description of the method, show an example of the method being used, and then show the output that that example would generate.

Remember that blocks are a way to pass *behavior* rather than data into methods. In each description, I'll use the phrase "Behavior X" to describe the behavior that might be passed to the method.

Method: times

Integers in Ruby can respond to a method called `times`. The `times` method accepts a block. The behavior in the block gets repeated *n* times, where *n* is the value of the integer on which `times` was called. In the example below we're calling `3.times`, which will repeat the behavior in the block three times.

The behavior of the `times` method could be described as: "however many times I specify, repeat Behavior X".

```
3.times do
  puts "hello"
end
```

Running this code will give the following output:

```
hello
hello
hello
```

Method: each

The `times` method's behavior is very simple. Whatever block it is given will be repeated in the exact same way each time it's executed. Not every block-taking method works this way. The `each` method passes an argument to its block each time the block is called. For instance, for the array `[1, 2, 3]`, the passed block will be called three times, first with 1 as the argument, then 2 on the second iteration, and finally with 3.

```
[1, 2, 3].each do |i|
  puts i
end
```

Output:

```
1
2
3
```

The `each method` could be described as "for each element in the given array, execute the given block, passing the element as an argument to the block."

Method: tap

First, here's what the code would look like without the `tap`.

```
require "tempfile"

def my_file
  file = Tempfile.new
  file.write("hello world")
  file.rewind
  file
end

puts my_file.read
```

"See this value? Perform Behavior X and then return that value."

Example: Initialize a file, write some content to it, then return the original file. (Behavior X is writing to the file.)

```
require "tempfile"

def my_file
  Tempfile.new.tap do |f|
    f.write("hello world")
    f.rewind
  end
end

puts my_file.read
```

Output:

```
hello world
```

Now let's look at how we can write our own method that can take a block.

10.2.2 Custom methods that take blocks

Every Ruby method, whether explicitly designed to or not, can take a block. Here's an example.

An HTML generator

The following method, inside_tag, does *not* take a block. It only takes a string argument which it will then output inside of a <p> tag.

```
def inside_tag(text)
  "<p>#{text}</p>"
end
```

This method might seem good enough. But what if we want to have more than one line of text inside our `<p>` tag? We can pass a string that contains a newline character (\n) but that would make the formatting look weird. If we call `inside_tag("line one\nline two")`, for example, the output would look like this:

```
<p>line one
line two<p>
```

Really we would prefer this:

```
<p>
  line one
  line two
<p>
```

Let's look at how we can make use of blocks to create a better HTML generator.

A better HTML generator

Here's a method which we can give an HTML tag as well as a piece of behavior. The method will execute our behavior. Before and after the behavior will be the opening and closing HTML tags.

```
inside_tag("p") do
  puts "Hello"
  puts "How are you?"
end
```

The output of this code looks like this.

```
<p>
Hello
How are you?
</p>
```

In this example, the "Behavior X" that we're passing to our method is printing the text "Hello" and then "How are you?".

Here's what the definition of such a method might look like.

```
def inside_tag(tag, &block)
  puts "<#{tag}>"   # output the opening tag
  block.call        # call the block that we were passed
  puts "</#{tag}>"  # output the closing tag
end
```

Our method has a weakness. The tag that the method outputs lacks indentation. We could of course add indentation by doing this:

```
puts "  Hello"
```

But that seems inelegant. How can we get our method to add indentation for us?

Adding an argument to the block

Let's now introduce a new object called Tag.

```
class Tag
  def content(value)
    puts "  #{value}"
  end
end
```

We can use Tag like this.

```
tag = Tag.new
tag.content "Hello"
```

This will output an indented string. Tag can be used in combination with our inside_tag method as follows.

```
def inside_tag(tag, &block)
  puts "<#{tag}>"
  block.call(Tag.new)
  puts "</#{tag}>"
end

inside_tag("p") do |tag|
  tag.content "Hello"
  tag.content "How are you?"
end
```

The above code gives the following output.

```
<p>
  Hello
  How are you?
</p>
```

Passing an object back to a block is a common DSL technique used in libraries like RSpec, Factory Bot, and Rails itself. Wherever you see respond_to in a Rails controller, for example, that's an instance of a block that gets an argument passed to it.

```
respond_to do |format|
  if @project.save
    format.html {
      redirect_to project_url(@project),
        notice: "Project was successfully created."
    }

    format.json {
      render :show, status: :created, location: @project
    }
  else
    format.html { render :new, status: :unprocessable_entity }

    format.json {
      render json: @project.errors, status: :unprocessable_entity
    }
  end
end
```

Compare `inside_tag("p") do |tag|` to `respond_to do |format|` and see if you can work out the ways in which they're similar to each other.

10.3   Proc Objects

You almost certainly use `Proc` objects all the time, even though you might not be aware of it. Blocks, which are ubiquitous in Ruby, and lambdas, which are used for things like Rails scopes, both involve `Proc` objects.

In this chapter, we're going to take a close look at `Proc` objects. First, we'll do a `Proc` object "hello world" to see what we're dealing with. Then we'll unpack the definition of `Proc` objects that the official Ruby docs give us. Lastly, we'll see how `Proc` objects relate to other concepts like blocks and lambdas.

10.3.1   A Proc object "hello world"

Before we talk about what `Proc` objects are and how they're used, let's take a look at a `Proc` object and mess around with it a little bit, just to see what one looks like and how it behaves.

The official Ruby docs provide a pretty good `Proc` object "hello world" example. Here it is:

```
square = Proc.new { |x| x**2 }
```

We can see how this `Proc` object works by opening up an `irb` console and defining the `Proc` object there. You may recognize from the Blocks section that the `Proc.new` method takes a block. We can invoke our new `Proc` object's block by calling `.call`.

```
> square = Proc.new { |x| x**2 }
 => #
> square.call(3)
 => 9
> square.call(4)
 => 16
> square.call(5)
 => 25
```

Now that we have a loose intuitive understanding, let's get a firmer grasp on what `Proc` objects are all about.

10.3.2   Understanding Proc objects more deeply

Blah

The official Ruby docs' definition of Proc objects

According to the official Ruby docs on Procs objects, "a Proc object is an encapsulation of a block of code, which can be stored in a local variable, passed to a method or another Proc, and can be called."

This definition is a bit of a mouthful. Let's take it a bit at a time to understand it better.

The Ruby Proc object definition, broken into chunks

A `Proc` object is:

- an encapsulation of a block of code

- which can be stored in a local variable

- or passed to a method or another Proc

- and can be called

Let's take these things one-by-one.

A Proc object is an encapsulation of a block of code. What might it mean for something to be an encapsulation of a block of code? In general, when you "encapsulate" something, you metaphorically put it in a capsule. Things that are in capsules are isolated from whatever's on the outside of the capsule. Encapsulating something also implies that it's "packaged up".

So when the docs say that a `Proc` object is "an encapsulation of a block of code", they must mean that the code in a `Proc` object is packaged up and isolated from the code outside it.

A Proc object can be stored in a local variable. For this one let's look at the same example from the docs:

```
square = Proc.new { |x| x**2 }
```

As we can see, this piece of code creates a `Proc` object and stores it in a local variable called `square`.

A Proc object can be passed to a method or another Proc. This one's a two-parter, so let's take each part individually. First let's focus on "A `Proc` object can be passed to another method".

Here's a method which can accept a `Proc` object. The first argument, `number`, just takes a number. The second argument, `operation`, takes a `Proc` object which can perform an operation on the number. Following the method are two `Proc` objects: `square`, which squares whatever number you give it, and `double`, which doubles whatever number you give it.

```
def perform_operation_on(number, operation)
  operation.call(number)
end
```

Here are a couple examples of `Proc` objects that could be plugged into `perform_operation_on`.

```
square = Proc.new { |x| x**2 }
double = Proc.new { |x| x * 2 }

puts perform_operation_on(5, square)
puts perform_operation_on(5, double)
```

Running this code gives the following output:

```
25
10
```

So that's what it means to pass a `Proc` object into a method. Instead of passing *data* as a method argument like normal, you can pass *behavior*. Or, to use some of the terminology from the `Proc` object definition, you can pass *an encapsulation of a block of code*. It's then up to that method to execute that encapsulated block of code whenever and however it sees fit.

We can even pass a `Proc` object into another `Proc` object. If we want to do that, the code looks pretty similar to our other example above.

```
perform_operation_on = Proc.new do |number, operation|
  operation.call(number)
end

square = Proc.new { |x| x**2 }
double = Proc.new { |x| x * 2 }

puts perform_operation_on.call(5, square)
puts perform_operation_on.call(5, double)
```

The only difference between this example and the one above it is that, in this example,
perform_operation_on is defined as a `Proc` object rather than a method. The ultimate behavior though is exactly the same.

A Proc object can be called   This last part of the definition of a `Proc` object, "a `Proc` object can be called", is perhaps obvious at this point but let's address it anyway for completeness' sake.

A `Proc` object can be called using the `#call` method, as follows.

```
square = Proc.new { |x| x**2 }
puts square.call(3)
```

Now let's look at the relationship between `Proc` objects and blocks.

10.3.3   Proc objects and blocks

Every block in Ruby is a `Proc` object, loosely speaking. Here's a custom method that accepts a block as an argument.

```
def my_method(&block)
  puts block.class
end

my_method { "hello" }
```

What's the class of the block we passed to my_method? We can run the code and see.

```
Proc
```

That's because the block we passed when calling my_method is a `Proc` object.

Below is an example that's functionally equivalent to the above. We've left the method itself alone and only changed the way we're calling it. The & in front of my_proc converts the `Proc` object into a block.

```
def my_method(&block)
  puts block.class
end

my_proc = Proc.new { "hello" }
my_method &my_proc
```

As we'll discuss more shortly, an & converts a `Proc` object to a block and vice-versa.

10.4   Closures

The concept of a closure is one that suffers from 1) an arguably misleading name (more about this soon) and 2) unhelpful, jargony explanations online.

My goal with this chapter is to provide an explanation of closures in plain language that can be understood by someone without a Computer Science background. And in fact, a Computer Science background is not needed, it's only the poor explanations of closures that make it seem so.

Let's dig deeper into what a closure actually is.

A closure is a record which stores a function plus (potentially) some variables. I'm going to break this definition into parts to help make it easier to understand.

- A closure is a record

- which stores a function

- plus (potentially) some variables

I'm going to discuss each part of this definition individually.

First, a reminder: the whole reason we're interested in Ruby closures is because of the Ruby concept of a Proc object, which is heavily involved in blocks. A `Proc` object is a closure. Therefore, all the examples of closures in this chapter will take the form of `Proc` objects.

10.4.1   First point: "A closure is a record"

A closure is a value that can be assigned to a variable or some other kind of "record". The term "record" doesn't have a special technical meaning here, we just use the word "record" because it's broader than "variable". Shortly we'll see an example of a closure being assigned to a record which is not a variable.

Here's a `Proc` object that's assigned to a variable.

```
my_proc = Proc.new { puts "I'm in a closure!" }
my_proc.call
```

Remember that every `Proc` object is a closure. When we do `Proc.new` we're creating a `Proc` object and thus a closure.

Here's another closure example. Here, instead of assigning the closure to a variable, we're assigning the closure to a key in a hash.

```
my_stuff = { my_proc: Proc.new { puts "I'm in a closure too!" } }
my_stuff[:my_proc].call
```

The point here is that the thing a closure gets assigned to isn't always a variable. That's why we say "record" and not "variable".

10.4.2 Second point: "which stores a function"

As you may have deduced, the code between the braces (puts "I'm in a closure!")
is the function we're talking about when we say "a closure is a record which stores
a function".

```
my_proc = Proc.new { puts "I'm in a closure!" }
my_proc.call
```

A closure can be thought of as a function "packed up" into a variable—or, more
precisely, a variable or some other kind of record.

10.4.3 Third point: "plus (potentially) some variables"

Here's a Proc object (which, again, is a closure) that involves an outside variable.

The variable number_of_exclamation_points gets included in the "environment" of the closure. Each time we call the closure that we've named amplifier,
the variable number_of_exclamation_points gets incremented and one additional exclamation point gets added to the string that gets output.

```
number_of_exclamation_points = 0

amplifier = Proc.new do
  number_of_exclamation_points += 1
  "louder" + ("!" * number_of_exclamation_points)
end

puts amplifier.call # louder!
puts amplifier.call # louder!!
puts amplifier.call # louder!!!
puts amplifier.call # louder!!!!
puts number_of_exclamation_points # 4 - the original variable was mutated
```

As a side note, I find the name "closure" to be misleading. The fact that the
above closure can mutate number_of_exclamation_points, a variable outside
the function's scope, seems to me like a decidedly *un*-closed idea. In fact, it seems
like there's a tunnel, an opening, between the closure and the outside scope, through
which changes can leak.

I personally started having an easy time understanding closures once I stopped
trying to connect the idea of "a closed thing" with how closures actually work.

10.5 The difference between procs and lambdas

If you've heard about procs you may also have heard about lambdas. What's the
difference between the two?

Lambdas actually *are* procs. Lambdas are just a special kind of proc and they behave a little bit differently from regular procs. In this section, we'll discuss the two main ways in which lambdas differ from regular procs:

1. The `return` keyword behaves differently

2. Arguments are handled differently

Let's take a look at each one of these differences in more detail.

10.5.1   The behavior of `return`

In lambdas, `return` means "exit from this lambda". In regular procs, `return` means "exit from embracing method".

Below is an example from the official Ruby docs which illustrates this difference.

```
def test_return
  # This is a lambda. The "return" just exits
  # from the lambda, nothing more.
  -> { return 3 }.call

  # This is a regular proc. The "return" returns
  # from the method, meaning control never reaches
  # the final "return 5" line.
  proc { return 4 }.call

  return 5
end

test_return # => 4
```

The other difference between procs and lambdas is how arguments are handled.

10.5.2   Argument handling

There are two ways in which procs and lambdas handle arguments differently.

Argument matching

A proc will happily execute a call with the wrong number of arguments. A lambda on the other hand requires all arguments to be present.

```
> p = proc { |x, y| "x is #{x} and y is #{y}" }
> p.call(1)
 => "x is 1 and y is "
> p.call(1, 2, 3)
 => "x is 1 and y is 2"
```

```
> l = lambda { |x, y| "x is #{x} and y is #{y}" }
> l.call(1)
(irb):5:in 'block in '. wrong number of arguments
  (given 1, expected 2) (ArgumentError)
> l.call(1, 2, 3)
(irb):14:in 'block in ': wrong number of arguments
  (given 3, expected 2) (ArgumentError)
```

In this way, lambdas are a bit more strict than procs.

Array deconstruction

If you call a proc with an array instead of separate arguments, the array will get deconstructed, as if the array is preceded with a splat operator.

```
> proc { |x, y| "x is #{x} and y is #{y}" }.call([1, 2])
 => "x is 1 and y is 2"
```

If you call a lambda with an array instead of separate arguments, the array will be interpreted as the first argument, and an `ArgumentError` will be raised because the second argument is missing.

```
> lambda { |x, y| "x is #{x} and y is #{y}" }.call([1, 2])
(irb):9:in 'block in ': wrong number of arguments
  (given 1, expected 2) (ArgumentError)
```

In other words, lambdas handle array deconstruction exactly like Ruby methods. Regular procs don't.

10.6 What the ampersand in front of &block means

```
def form_for(record, options = {}, &block)
```

The first two arguments, `record` and `options = {}`, are straightforward to someone who's familiar with Ruby. But the third argument, `&block`, is a little more mysterious. Why the leading ampersand?

In order to begin to understand what the leading ampersand is all about, let's review how blocks relate to `Proc` objects.

10.6.1 Blocks and Proc objects

Let's talk about blocks and `Proc` objects a little bit, starting with `Proc` objects.

Here's a method which takes an argument. The method doesn't care of what type the argument is. All the method does is output the argument's class.

After we define the method, we call the method and pass it a `Proc` object.

```
def proc_me(my_proc)
  puts my_proc.class
end

proc_me(Proc.new { puts "hi" })
```

If you run this code, the output will be:

```
Proc
```

Not too surprising. We're passing a `Proc` object as an argument to the `proc_me` method. Naturally, it thinks that `my_proc` is a `Proc` object.

Now let's add another method, `block_me`, which accepts a block.

```
def proc_me(my_proc)
  puts my_proc.class
end

def block_me(&my_block)
  puts my_block.class
end

proc_me(Proc.new { puts "hi" })
block_me { puts "hi" }
```

If we run this code the output will be:

```
Proc
Proc
```

Even though we're passing a `Proc` object the first time and a block the second time, we see `Proc` for both lines.

The reason that the result of `my_block.class` is `Proc` is because **a leading ampersand converts a block to a Proc object**.

10.6.2 Converting the Proc object to a block before passing the Proc object

Here's a slightly altered version of the above example. Notice how `my_proc` has changed to `&my_proc`. The other change is that `Proc.new` has changed to `&Proc.new`.

```
def proc_me(&my_proc) # an & was added here
  puts my_proc.class
end

def block_me(&my_block)
  puts my_block.class
```

```
end
```

```
proc_me(&Proc.new { puts "hi" }) # an & was added here
block_me { puts "hi" }
```

If we run this code the output is the exact same.

```
Proc
Proc
```

This is because not only does a leading ampersand convert a block to a Proc object, but a leading ampersand also converts a Proc object to a block.

10.7 The two common ways to call a Ruby block

In this section, we'll go over the two most common ways of calling a Ruby block: `block.call` and `yield`.

There are also other ways to call a block, e.g., `instance_exec`. But that's an "advanced" topic which I'll leave out of the scope of this section.

Here are the two common ways of calling a Ruby block and why they exist.

10.7.1 The first way: block.call

Below is a method that accepts a block, then calls that block.

```
def hello(&block)
  block.call
end
```

```
hello { puts "hey!" }
```

If you run this code, you'll see the output `hey!`.

As we've seen, the `&` converts the block into a Proc object. The block can't be called directly using `.call`. The block has to be converted into a `Proc` object first and then `.call` is called on the `Proc` object.

10.7.2 The second way: yield

The example below is very similar to the first example, except instead of using `block.call` we're using `yield`.

```
def hello(&block)
  yield
end
```

```
hello { puts "hey!" }
```

You may wonder: if we already have `block.call`, why does Ruby provide a second, slightly different way of calling a block?

One reason is that `yield` gives us a capability that `block.call` doesn't have. In the below example, we define a method and then pass a block to it, but we never have to explicitly specify that the method takes a block.

```
def hello
  yield
end
```

```
hello { puts "hey!" }
```

As you can see, `yield` gives us the ability to call a block even if our method doesn't explicitly take a block. (Side note: *any* Ruby method can be passed a block, even if the method doesn't explicitly take one.)

The fact that `yield` exists raises the question: why not just use `yield` all the time?

The answer is that when you use `block.call`, you have the ability to pass the block to another method if you so choose, which is something you can't do with `yield`.

When we put `&block` in a method's signature, we can do more with the block than just call it using `block.call`. We could also, for example, choose *not* to call the block but rather pass the block to a different method which then calls the block.

10.8   How instance_exec works

Ruby's `instance_exec` method can be used to clean up certain noisy parts of a DSL.

10.8.1   Passing arguments to blocks

When calling a Ruby block using `block.call`, you can pass an argument (e.g., `block.call("hello")`) and the argument will be fed to the block.

Here's an example of passing an argument when calling a block.

```
def word_fiddler(&block)
  block.call("hello")
end
```

```
word_fiddler do |word|
  puts word.upcase
end
```

In this case, the string "hello" gets passed for `word`, and `word.upcase` outputs HELLO.

We can use a method called `instance_exec` to execute our block in the *context* of whatever argument we send it.

10.8.2 Executing a block in a different context

Note how in the following example `word.upcase` has changed to just `upcase`.

```
def word_fiddler(&block)
  "hello".instance_exec(&block)
end

word_fiddler do
  puts upcase
end
```

The behavior is the exact same. The output is identical. The only difference is how the behavior is expressed in the code.

10.8.3 How this works

Every command in Ruby operates in a **context**. Every context is an object. The default context is an object called `main`, which you can demonstrate by opening a Ruby console and typing `self`.

We can also demonstrate this for our earlier `word_fiddler` snippet.

```
def word_fiddler(&block)
  block.call("hello")
end

word_fiddler do |word|
  puts self # shows the current context
  puts word.upcase
end
```

If you run the above snippet, you'll see the following output:

```
main
HELLO
```

The `instance_exec` method works because it **changes the context of the block it invokes**. Here's our `instance_exec` snippet with a `puts self` line added.

```
def word_fiddler(&block)
  "hello".instance_exec(&block)
end
```

```
word_fiddler do
  puts self
  puts upcase
end
```

Instead of `main`, we now get `hello`.

10.8.4   Why instance_exec is useful

The `instance_exec` method can help make Ruby DSLs less verbose.
   Consider the following Factory Bot snippet:

```
FactoryBot.define do
  factory :user do
    first_name { 'John' }
    last_name { 'Smith' }
  end
end
```

The code above consists of two blocks, one nested inside the other. There are
three methods called in the snippet, or more precisely, there are three *messages*
being sent: `factory`, `first_name`, and `last_name`.
   Who is the recipient of these messages? It's not the default context, `main`. The
syntax would be pretty verbose and noisy without the ability to change blocks'
contexts using `instance_exec`.

10.9   How and why to use method_missing

Normally, an object only responds to messages that match the names of the object's methods and public accessors. `method_missing` allows objects to respond
to messages that don't correspond to existing methods or accessors, enhancing flexibility, especially in scenarios like dynamic attribute access or constructing Domain
Specific Languages (DSLs).

10.9.1   Arbitrary attribute setter example

To illustrate, consider an example where we use `method_missing` to dynamically
set attribute values on a `User` object.

A plain User object

Initially, our `User` class is empty, lacking a `set_first_name` method:

```
class User
end

user = User.new
user.set_first_name("Jason")
```

Attempting to call set_first_name results in a NoMethodError.

Adding method_missing

We implement method_missing to catch undefined method calls, allowing dynamic handling:

```
class User
  def method_missing(method_name, *args)
    puts method_name
    puts args
  end
end

user = User.new
user.set_first_name("Jason")
```

This setup prints the method name and arguments, demonstrating how method_missing intercepts the call.

Parsing the attribute name

Next, we parse the attribute name from the method call for more specific handling:

```
class User
  def method_missing(method_name, value)
    attr_name = method_name.to_s[4..]
    puts attr_name
  end
end

user = User.new
user.set_first_name("Jason")
```

This code snippet extracts and prints the attribute name, first_name.

Setting the attribute

Finally, we use instance_variable_set to dynamically set the attribute value:

```ruby
class User
  def method_missing(method_name, *args)
    attr_name = method_name.to_s[4..]
    instance_variable_set("@#{attr_name}", args[0])
  end
end

user = User.new
user.set_first_name("Jason")
puts user.instance_variable_get("@first_name")
```

This code sets and retrieves the value Jason for the first_name attribute, showcasing a practical use of method_missing for dynamic attribute handling.

Chapter 11

Factory Bot

Factory Bot is a library to assist with test data creation. How is using Factory Bot better than creating test data manually in tests?

Abstraction is the art of hiding distracting details and emphasizing essential information. In test data, it's often the case that some parts of the data are significant and other parts are only filler. For example, if I want to assert that no two hair salon clients can have an appointment with the same stylist at the same time, then I may want my setup data to include two appointments that conflict. It would be helpful for the test to show that the two appointments have the same stylist and start time, since those attributes are significant to the scenario, but it wouldn't be helpful, in fact it would be unhelpful, for the test to show insignificant details like the client's contact information.

Here's an example of a test without Factory Bot. Because all the records are created manually, no required fields can be left blank.

```
RSpec.describe Appointment, type: :model do
  context "booking an appointment when another appointment already" \
          "exists for the same stylist at the same time" do
    it "is not valid" do
      griselda = Stylist.create!(
        name: "Griselda",
        email: "griselda@example.com"
      )

      greg = Client.create!(
        name: "Greg",
        phone: "123-456-7890",
        email: "greg@example.com"
      )

      Appointment.create!(
        stylist: griselda,
        start_time: "2020-01-01 08:00:00",
```

```
      client: greg
    )

    nebuchadnezzar = Client.create!(
      name: "Nebuchadnezzar", phone: "987-654-3210",
      email: "nebuchadnezzar_7@example.com"
    )

    conflicting_appointment = Appointment.new(
      stylist: griselda,
      start_time: "2020-01-01 08:00:00",
      client: nebuchadnezzar
    )

    expect(conflicting_appointment.valid?).to eq(false)
  end
  end
end
```

Here's the same test again, but using Factory Bot.

```
RSpec.describe Appointment, type: :model do
  context "booking an appointment when another appointment already" \
          "exists for the same stylist at the same time" do
    it "is not valid" do
      griselda = FactoryBot.create(:stylist)

      FactoryBot.create(
        :appointment,
        start_time: "2020-01-01 08:00:00",
        stylist: griselda
      )

      conflicting_appointment = FactoryBot.build(
        :appointment,
        start_time: "2020-01-01 08:00:00",
        stylist: griselda
      )

      expect(conflicting_appointment.valid?).to eq(false)
    end
  end
end
```

In the second test, the irrelevant details are hidden away while the essential information is emphasized. We shouldn't have to care what the stylist's email address is. We *certainly* shouldn't have to care what Greg's email address is. In fact, we shouldn't even have to care who the client is for each appointment. (This example assumes that the client factory is configured to generate a fresh, unique client for each new appointment.)

We do, however, want to make it clear that both appointments are for the same stylist. (Why call the stylist `griselda` rather than just `stylist`? Because it's easier to see the unique name of `griselda` repeated a few times in the test than see `stylist` and remember what `stylist` means. Concrete examples are easier to understand than abstract ones.)

We also want to make it obvious that both appointments start at the same time. The reason for hard-coding and duplicating the start time is the same reason we named the stylist `griselda` instead of just `stylist`: concrete examples are easier to understand than abstract ones.

11.1 Installation

Since Factory Bot is a third-party library that doesn't come with Rails, we'll have to install it.

Actually, there's a special variation of the Factory Bot library which, unlike the standard version, is tailored specifically to Rails. To install the library, add the `factory_bot_rails` gem to the `:development, :test` group of your Gemfile.

```
group :development, :test do
  gem 'factory_bot_rails'
end
```

Run `bundle install` afterward to install the gem.

11.2 Defining factories

```
FactoryBot.define do
  factory :user do
    first_name { 'John' }
    last_name { 'Smith' }
    email { 'john.smith@example.com' }
  end
end
```

This factory maps to the `User` model and specifies default values for its attributes.

11.3 Where to put factory definitions

The most popular place to put factory definitions is in `spec/factories`, with one file for each factory. This is mostly fine but it does come with some drawbacks. To me, the main problem with having one file per factory is that inevitably some of your factories end up "footing someone else's bill". In the beginning of a project, factories are easy to keep tidy because there's hardly anything in them. As the project grows, factories end up collecting miscellaneous bits and pieces. The more "important" a model is, the more stuff will end up in that model's factory, and eventually the factory will become a convoluted mess.

In Chapter 5 we saw the heretical idea of organizing a test suite by domain concept rather than test type.

11.4   Factory Bot hello world

Here's an example of how to create a factory in a fresh Rails app. First, in order to skip a little tedious and irrelevant setup work, you can use a Rails application template I've set up for readers of this book.

```
$ rails new factory_bot_hello_world -T -d postgresql \
  -m https://raw.githubusercontent.com/\
jasonswett/testing_application_template/\
master/application_template.rb
```

In order to have a working factory, we have to have a Rails model for the factory to match up to. Let's generate a model called `User` with three attributes: `first_name`, `last_name` and `email`.

```
$ rails g scaffold user first_name:string last_name:string email:string
```

Place the following code in `spec/factories/users.rb`. (You'll have to create the `spec/factories` directory first.)

```
# spec/factories/users.rb

FactoryBot.define do
  factory :user do
    first_name { 'John' }
    last_name { 'Smith' }
    email { 'john.smith@example.com' }
  end
end
```

Now our factory is ready to be used. Here's an example of how we can do so.

```
$ rails console
> FactoryBot.create(:user)
```

11.5   Using Factory Bot inside an RSpec test

Now that we've seen an example of how to create and use a factory, let's look at
how to use a factory inside an RSpec test.

```
RSpec.describe User do
  describe "#full_name" do
    it "concatenates first and last name" do
      user = FactoryBot.create(
        :user,
        first_name: "Ringo",
        last_name: "Starr"
      )

      expect(user.full_name).to eq("Ringo Starr")
    end
  end
end
```

We don't need to do anything special in order for our factories to be available
in our tests. RSpec will see the factory definitions and include them automatically.

11.6   Configuring Factory Bot with RSpec

To simplify syntax in RSpec tests, include the following configuration in
`spec/rails_helper.rb`.

```
RSpec.configure do |config|
  config.include FactoryBot::Syntax::Methods
end
```

This allows using `create(:user)` instead of `FactoryBot.create(:user)`,
as in the example below.

```
RSpec.describe User do
  describe "#full_name" do
    it "concatenates first and last name" do
      user = create(
        :user,
        first_name: "Ringo",
        last_name: "Starr"
      )

      expect(user.full_name).to eq("Ringo Starr")
    end
  end
end
```

Since most tests include some setup data, `FactoryBot` ends up appearing many many times in our tests. This just creates distracting noise. By configuring Factory Bot to let us use the bare `create` and `build` methods instead of `FactoryBot.create` and `FactoryBot.build`, we can cut down on this noise.

11.7   Build strategies

Sometimes, in a test, you need an instance of a model with a persisted database record behind it. Other times you just need an instance of a model in memory with some attributes filled in with realistic values. Consider, for example, the scenario below, where we want to assert that a user with a duplicate email address is not valid.

```
RSpec.describe User do
  context "user has a non-unique email address" do
    it "is not valid" do
      create(:user, email: "ringo@example.com")

      user = build(:user, email: "ringo@example.com")
      expect(user).not_to be_valid
    end
  end
end
```

We want the first of the two users to be persisted to the database because that's where a uniqueness validation will look to see if its value is unique. With the second user, not only do we not want the record to be persisted to the database, but we can't, because the email uniqueness validator won't allow the record to be saved.

That's why Factory Bot offers two main methods for creating objects: `create` and `build`. `create` returns a persisted instance of a model, while `build` returns an unpersisted instance. This distinction allows for flexibility in testing, depending on whether a persisted or unpersisted object is needed.

Here's a reminder of our factory definition:

```
FactoryBot.define do
  factory :user do
    first_name { 'John' }
    last_name { 'Smith' }
    email { 'john.smith@example.com' }
  end
end
```

Using `create` results in a persisted `User` object, while `build` gives you a new, unpersisted `User` object:

```
> user = FactoryBot.create(:user)
> user.persisted? # true
> user.id # an ID value

> user = FactoryBot.build(:user)
> user.persisted? # false
> user.id # nil
```

The `build` method also confers a performance advantage: the fewer times your test suite hits the database, the faster the tests will be. It's generally a good idea to use `build` when you can get away with it and `create` only when you truly need a persisted record.

11.8   Using Factory Bot with Faker

The examples we've seen so far have used hard-coded values like "john.smith@example.com". That's often fine, but there are certain reasons we wouldn't always want to use hard-coded values.

```
FactoryBot.define do
  factory :user do
    first_name { 'John' }
    last_name { 'Smith' }
    email { Faker::Internet.email }
  end
end
```

This approach utilizes `Faker::Internet.email` to generate unique and realistic email addresses, improving the elegance and maintainability of factory definitions.

Here's an example of a full `User` factory with all attributes utilizing Faker:

```
FactoryBot.define do
  factory :user do
    first_name { Faker::Name.first_name }
    last_name { Faker::Name.last_name }
    email { Faker::Internet.email }
  end
end
```

The integration of Faker with Factory Bot significantly enhances the realism and utility of test data, making for more meaningful tests.

11.9   Nested factories

Sometimes it's helpful to have a reusable variation on a factory. For example, I
once worked on an app where I had a frequent need to generate user records with
a role of "physician". I didn't want to have to tediously set the `role` attribute to
"physician" in the dozens of places where I needed it, nor did I want to add the role
of "physician" to the main `User` factory, since the physicial role was not appropriate
most of the time.

```
FactoryBot.define do
  factory :user do
    username { Faker::Internet.username }
    password { Faker::Internet.password }

    factory :physician_user do
      role { "physician" }
    end
  end
end
```

When it's needed, a nested factory can be used just like any other factory.

```
> physician_user = FactoryBot.create(:physician_user)
> physician_user.role
"physician"
```

Using nested factories allows us to avoid needless repetition in tests while also
allowing the parent factory to maintain cohesion.

11.10   Traits

A nested factory is an "is a" relationship. A physician user, for example, is a user.
Traits are a "has a" relationship. In the examples below, the `:with_name` trait and
the `:with_ssn` trait give the user a "has a name" and "has an SSN" property.

```
FactoryBot.define do
  factory :user do
    username { Faker::Internet.username }
    password { Faker::Internet.password }

    trait :with_name do
      first_name { "John" }
      last_name { "Smith" }
    end

    trait :with_ssn do
```

```
      ssn { "123-45-6789" }
    end
  end
end
```

Traits can be invoked as follows:

```
# Using one trait at a time
FactoryBot.create(:user, :with_name)
FactoryBot.create(:user, :with_ssn)

# Using multiple traits at once
FactoryBot.create(:user, :with_name, :with_ssn)
```

Traits have a similar benefit to nested factories in that they help keep tests DRY while also allowing factories to maintain cohesion. Whether to use nested factories or traits depends on whether you want an is-a or a has-a relationship.

11.11   Callbacks

In the `physician_user` example we saw earlier, the need we were addressing was to repeatedly set the `role` attribute to "physician". What if our need is something else, like creating a certain record? In these cases we can use *callbacks*.

```
FactoryBot.define do
  factory :user do
    username { Faker::Internet.username }
    password { Faker::Internet.password }

    factory :user_with_message do
      after(:create) do |user|
        create(:message, user: user)
      end
    end
  end
end
```

Invoke `FactoryBot.create(:user_with_message)` to automatically associate a message with the user.

11.12   Transient attributes

Consider the following test, which creates an "insurance deposit" with a PDF attachment. The assertions have been omitted; all that's shown is the setup.

```
RSpec.describe InsuranceDeposit, type: :model do
  before do
    insurance_deposit = create(:insurance_deposit)

    file = Tempfile.new(["insurance", ".pdf"])
    Prawn::Document.generate(file.path) do |pdf|
      pdf.text "This is a test PDF file."
    end

    insurance_deposit.pdf_files.attach(
      io: File.open(file.path),
      filename: "test.pdf",
      content_type: "application/pdf"
    )
  end
end
```

That's a lot of noise. It would be so much nicer if we could abstract away the details and just do something like this:

```
RSpec.describe InsuranceDeposit, type: :model do
  before do
    insurance_deposit = create(
      :insurance_deposit,
      pdf_content: "my arbitrary PDF content"
    )
  end
```

This is possible through *transient attributes*, a feature which provides a way to pass arbitrary values to factories when generating records. Below is how we could modify the insurance_deposit factory to include a transient attribute called pdf_content.

```
FactoryBot.define do
  factory :insurance_deposit do
    transient do
      pdf_content { "" }
    end

    after(:create) do |insurance_deposit, evaluator|
      file = Tempfile.new
      pdf = Prawn::Document.new
      pdf.text evaluator.pdf_content
      pdf.render_file file.path

      insurance_deposit.pdf_files.attach(
        io: File.open(file.path),
        filename: "file.pdf"
```

```
      )
    end
  end
end
```

By moving the details below the surface, we can keep our tests at a higher level of abstraction, making them easier to understand and maintain.

Chapter 12

RSpec syntax

When you first see RSpec syntax, you might find it very mysterious. What crazy magic allows syntax like this? Where does the Ruby stop and the RSpec start? Which parts are RSpec and which parts are Rails? Which parts are significant and which parts are arbitrary?

In this chapter we'll take a close look at RSpec syntax and why it is the way it is, building on what we've seen in Chapter 17, Ruby DSLs.

12.1 An RSpec test, dissected

We're going to thoroughly demystify RSpec syntax by picking apart an example.

```
RSpec.describe "name reverser" do
  it "reverses a name" do
    expect(reverse_name("John Lennon")).to eq("Lennon, John")
  end
end
```

The name RSpec stands for *Ruby specification*. The library is called RSpec and not RTest because the author of the library wanted to convey (just like I do in chapter 2) that tests can be thought of as executable specifications. In RSpec terminology, we don't write tests, we write specifications, or specs for short. In this chapter and elsewhere in the book I choose to be sloppy and use the terms "test" and "spec" interchangeably. When you see a reference to a "spec", just know that it merely means "test" and nothing more.

12.1.1 Examples and example groups

In our name reverser spec, the portion inside the `it` block is known an *example*. Our program has specifications, and we illustrate these specifications through examples.

Often it's helpful to organize examples into groups. The term for this is, natually, *example group*. Below is an example which we first saw in chapter 2. In this file, there are two examples ("it assigns the multiplication operator to the root" and "it assigns the first operand to the left child") organized into a single group, labeled "the expression involves multiplication with an explicit operator".

```ruby
RSpec.describe "expression parser" do
  context "the expression involves multiplication with" \
    "an explicit operator" do
    it "assigns the multiplication operator to the root" do
      expression = Expression.parse("2*x")
expect(expression.root).to eq("*")
    end

    it "assigns the first operand to the left child" do
      expression = Expression.parse("2*x")
      expect(expression.left_child).to eq(2)
    end
  end
end
```

Below is another example. This one has two example groups, one for "before a job has finished" and another for "when a job finishes". In this case each "group" actually contains only one example. The groups are simply being used to make a distinction between two different scenarios.

```ruby
RSpec.describe "Charges", type: :system do
  context "before a job has finished" do
    let!(:job) { create(:job) }

    it "does not have a charge" do
      expect(job.charge).to be nil
    end
  end

  context "when a job finishes" do
    let!(:job) { create(:job) }

    before do
      allow(Rails.configuration)
        .to receive(:charge_rate).and_return(0.2)

      job.finish!
    end

    it "captures the charge rate at that point in time" do
      expect(job.charge.rate).to eq(0.2)
```

```
      end
    end
end
```

A block can be denoted either by `context` or `describe`. There's no functional difference between the two. Whether to use `context` or `describe` in any particular case is an arbitrary judgment call for the human writer of the test. Here's a test where I used `describe` instead of `context` because I found `describe` to be more fitting.

```
RSpec.describe "one failing job" do
  let!(:build) { create(:build) }

  let!(:passing_job) do
    create(:job, build:, order_index: 0)
  end

  let!(:failing_job) do
    create(:job, build:, order_index: 1, test_report: "failed")
  end

  describe "build status" do
    it "gets set to 'Failed'" do
      passing_job.finish!
      failing_job.finish!
      expect(build.reload.cached_status).to eq("Failed")
    end
  end
end
```

Syntactically, an example group is a method that takes a block. To make it more clear that `describe` and `context` are just methods, here's what an example group would look like with parentheses added. In fact, we can do the same thing with `it` because `it` is a method too.

```
describe("build status") do
  it("gets set to 'Failed'") do
    passing_job.finish!
    failing_job.finish!
    expect(build.reload.cached_status).to eq("Failed")
  end
end
```

12.1.2 The expect keyword

Every test has at least one *assertion*. We assert that something is true, and if it's not, the test fails. Test frameworks like Minitest use the `assert` keyword for assertions, but RSpec does it a little bit differently. In an assertion like the following, RSpec uses a combination of `expect` and `eq` to assert that a certain condition is true.

```
expect(build.reload.cached_status).to eq("Failed")
```

The `expect` part, which signifies the value we want to perform an assertion on, is always the some. The `expect` keyword is used in combination with a *matcher*, which is most commonly `eq` (equals) but can be any number of things.

12.1.3   The eq matcher

The syntax of `.to eq()` often looks strange and arbitrary to RSpec beginners. Much of the RSpec syntax (which we'll see a lot more of soon) can look like a soup of dots, spaces and underscores, with no apparent rhyme or reason as to what's what. Luckily, I assure you that this confusion goes away as you get more familiar with what the RSpec DSL is made of and as you get practice writing RSpec tests.

For the `.to` part of `expect(expression.root).to eq("*")`, it helps to recognize that `to` is just a method. In fact, we can add the missing optional parentheses on the `to` method to make it clearer that `to` is just a method.

```
expect(expression.root).to(eq("*"))
```

`eq` is also a method. The argument that we pass to the `to` method is `eq("*")`, so in other words, whatever the return value of `eq("*")` is, is what gets passed to `to`. What's the return value of `eq("*")`?

Well, `eq("*")` returns an instance of a class called `RSpec::Matchers::BuiltIn::Eq`. By looking at the source code for `RSpec::Matchers::BuiltIn::Eq`, we can see that it has a method called `expected` that works like this:

```
eq("*").expected
# returns "*"
```

Presumably, the `to` method in `expect(expression.root).to(eq("*"))` expects to get an instance of `RSpec::Matchers::BuiltIn::Eq` (or other matcher class) as an argument, and calls the `expected` method on that object which returns whatever was passed to `eq`.

12.1.4   What's next

What we're going to do now is something that I hope will make the RSpec syntax even less mysterious to you, which is that we're going to write our own RSpec-like test framework from scratch.

12.2   Build your own RSpec

In this section we're going to build our own RSpec-like test framework called
MySpec. By the end of this section you'll be able to run the following test file.

```
require_relative './my_spec'

def emphasize(text)
  "#{text.upcase}!"
end

# Above this line is the "application code"
# and below this line is the test code
# ---------------------------------------

MySpec.describe 'emphasizing text' do
  it 'makes the text uppercase and adds an exclamation point' do
    expect(emphasize('hello')).to eq('HELLO!')
  end
end
```

Let's begin the implementation.

12.2.1   Step 1: expect

We'll break off a small chunk of the job and address that first, starting with the
innermost part of the test, the expectation.

For convenience, we'll include the "application code" (i.e. the `emphasize`
method) right in the same file as the test code.

```
def emphasize(text)
  "#{text.upcase}!"
end

expect(emphasize('hello')).to eq('HELLO!')
```

Throughout this process, we're going to use the method of "error-driven development" (not a real thing, just something I made up). We'll write some code, run
the code, see what errors we get, fix the errors, and repeat.

You can execute the above code with the following command.

```
$ ruby emphasize_spec.rb
```

Beginning the process

If we execute this file now, we get the following error.

```
emphasize_spec.rb:5:in '<main>': undefined method 'expect' for
  main:Object (NoMethodError)
```

The error is telling us `expect` is an undefined method, which is true. We haven't defined a method called `expect` yet. Let's define it.

```
def emphasize(text)
  "#{text.upcase}!"
end

def expect(things)
end

expect(emphasize('hello')).to eq('HELLO!')
```

Now, if we execute the file again, we get a different error.

```
emphasize_spec.rb:8:in '<main>': undefined method 'eq' for
  main:Object (NoMethodError)
```

This time `eq` isn't defined. Let's define that method as well.

```
def emphasize(text)
  "#{text.upcase}!"
end

def expect(things)
end

def eq(thing)
end

expect(emphasize('hello')).to eq('HELLO!')
```

Now that both `expect` and `eq` are defined, we get another error.

```
emphasize_spec.rb:11:in '<main>': undefined method 'to' for
  nil:NilClass (NoMethodError)
```

This one is perhaps less straightforward, so I'll explain what's happening. This error means that the object we're calling `to` on is `nil`.

We're calling `to` on `expect(emphasize('hello'))`, so it must be that the return value of
`expect(emphasize('hello'))` is `nil`.

This is indeed the case. When we defined `expect`, we didn't put a body in the method definition, so the return value of `expect` is `nil`.

To fix this error, we need to change `expect` from returning `nil` to returning an object that will respond to a method called `to`. The only mystery is exactly what we should return.

```
def expect(things)
  # something needs to go here...but what?
end
```

In this case we can look to RSpec for guidance. The real `expect` method in RSpec returns an object of type `RSpec::Expectations::ExpectationTarget`. Maybe we can create our own `ExpectationTarget` class and have `expect` return an instance of it.

```
def emphasize(text)
  "#{text.upcase}!"
end

class ExpectationTarget
end

def expect(things)
  ExpectationTarget.new
end

def eq(thing)
end

expect(emphasize('hello')).to eq('HELLO!')
```

Now we get a different error.

```
emphasize_spec.rb:15:in '<main>': undefined method 'to'
for #<ExpectationTarget:0x00007fe3020271b8> (NoMethodError)
```

This is unsurprising. We haven't defined `ExpectationTarget#to`, so of course the method is going to be undefined. Let's add `to`.

```
def emphasize(text)
  "#{text.upcase}!"
end

class ExpectationTarget
  def to(thing)
  end
end

def expect(things)
  ExpectationTarget.new
end

def eq(thing)
```

```
end

expect(emphasize('hello')).to(eq('HELLO!'))
```

Now we get no errors when we run the file, although nothing happens. Let's make it so that if the test passes, it outputs a dot, and if the test fails, it raises an exception.

```
def emphasize(text)
  "#{text.upcase}!"
end

class ExpectationTarget
  def initialize(output)
    @output = output
  end

  def to(expected_output)
    if @output == expected_output
      puts '.'
    else
      raise "Expected #{@output} to equal #{expected_output}"
    end
  end
end

def expect(output)
  ExpectationTarget.new(output)
end

def eq(expected_output)
  expected_output
end

expect(emphasize('hello')).to(eq('HELLO!'))
```

If we run the file now we see an output of just a dot (.). This is because our expected output, HELLO!, does indeed match the actual output. We can see the failure output if we change HELLO! to something incorrect, like goodbye.

```
expect(emphasize('hello')).to(eq('goodbye'))
```

Now we get:

```
emphasize_spec.rb:14:in 'to': Expected HELLO! to equal goodbye
(RuntimeError)
```

We now have something that vaguely resembles a working RSpec test!

12.2.2 Organizing our files

Right now everything is all in one file. It's getting a little hard to read. Let's take all our "library code" and move it into a separate file, my_spec.rb.

```
class ExpectationTarget
  def initialize(output)
    @output = output
  end

  def to(expected_output)
    if @output == expected_output
      puts '.'
    else
      raise "Expected #{@output} to equal #{expected_output}"
    end
  end
end

def expect(output)
  ExpectationTarget.new(output)
end

def eq(expected_output)
  expected_output
end
```

What's left will stay in emphasize_spec.rb. We'll need to add one line to require the my_spec.rb file.

```
require_relative './my_spec'

def emphasize(text)
  "#{text.upcase}!"
end

expect(emphasize('hello')).to eq('HELLO!')
```

12.2.3 More closely matching RSpec syntax

Now let's make our syntax more closely match the real RSpec syntax.

```
MySpec.describe 'emphasizing text' do
  it 'makes the text uppercase and adds an exclamation point' do
    expect(emphasize('hello')).to eq('HELLO!')
  end
end
```

In addition to our expect, we're going to have surrounding it and describe blocks, like the above.

In the last section we got as far as re-implementing RSpec's expect, to and eq.

```
require_relative './my_spec'

def emphasize(text)
  "#{text.upcase}!"
end

expect(emphasize('hello')).to eq('HELLO!')
```

Now let's make our test look even more like a real RSpec test by implementing describe and it.

```
require_relative './my_spec'

def emphasize(text)
  "#{text.upcase}!"
end

MySpec.describe 'emphasizing text' do
  it 'makes the text uppercase and adds an exclamation point' do
    expect(emphasize('hello')).to eq('HELLO!')
  end
end
```

We'll start with just the inner part, the it block.

```
it 'makes the text uppercase and adds an exclamation point' do
  expect(emphasize('hello')).to eq('HELLO!')
end
```

12.2.4   The implementation

First let's surround the expect line with an it block.

```
require_relative './my_spec'

def emphasize(text)
  "#{text.upcase}!"
end

it 'makes the text uppercase and adds an exclamation point' do
  expect(emphasize('hello')).to(eq('HELLO!'))
end
```

Now, if we run `emphasize_spec.rb`, we get the following error. The `it` method we referred to is of course undefined.

```
emphasize_spec.rb:27:in '<main>': undefined method 'it' for
  main:Object (NoMethodError)
```

Let's add an `it` method which does nothing but `yield` whatever block is passed to it.

```ruby
def emphasize(text)
  "#{text.upcase}!"
end

class ExpectationTarget
  def initialize(output)
    @output = output
  end

  def to(expected_output)
    if @output == expected_output
      puts '.'
    else
      raise "Expected #{@output} to equal #{expected_output}"
    end
  end
end

def expect(output)
  ExpectationTarget.new(output)
end

def eq(expected_output)
  expected_output
end

def it(description)
  yield
end
```

Now if we run the file, the test will execute as expected. The `it` block doesn't actually need to do anything, it's just a wrapper for the benefit of the human reader.

Adding the outer block

Let's now wrap our test in `MySpec.describe` as shown below.

```ruby
require_relative './my_spec'
```

```
def emphasize(text)
  "#{text.upcase}!"
end

MySpec.describe 'emphasizing text' do
  it 'makes the text uppercase and adds an exclamation point' do
    expect(emphasize('hello')).to(eq('HELLO!'))
  end
end
```

If we run our file, it will of course fail because MySpec is undefined.

```
emphasize_spec.rb:31:in '<main>': uninitialized constant
  MySpec (NameError)
```

Let's add a MySpec class to make this particular error go away.

```
class MySpec
end

class ExpectationTarget
  def initialize(output)
    @output = output
  end

  def to(expected_output)
    if @output == expected_output
      puts '.'
    else
      raise "Expected #{@output} to equal #{expected_output}"
    end
  end
end

def expect(output)
  ExpectationTarget.new(output)
end

def eq(expected_output)
  expected_output
end

def it(description)
  yield
end
```

If we run the file now, the error about MySpec goes away, but we get an error saying (correctly of course) that there's no `describe` method on the MySpec class.

```
emphasize_spec.rb:34:in '<main>': undefined method 'describe'
  for MySpec:Class (NoMethodError)
```

Let's add a `describe` method which, like the `it` method we defined, will simply `yield` whatever block is passed to it.

```
class MySpec
  def self.describe(description)
    yield
  end
end

class ExpectationTarget
  def initialize(output)
    @output = output
  end

  def to(expected_output)
    if @output == expected_output
      puts '.'
    else
      raise "Expected #{@output} to equal #{expected_output}"
    end
  end
end

def expect(output)
  ExpectationTarget.new(output)
end

def eq(expected_output)
  expected_output
end

def it(description)
  yield
end
```

Now everything works, and we now have a complete test that very much resembles an RSpec test!

This concludes the build your own RSpec section. In the next section we'll examine two important RSpec keywords: `describe` and `context`.

12.3 Describe and context

The `describe` and `context` keywords are just aliases for one another. Mechanically, they're 100% equivalent. The only reason the two keywords exist is for the benefit of the human reader.

12.3.1   When I use describe

I tend to use `describe` when I'm describing a method or a feature. If I were to write a test for a method called `first_name`, I might write it something like this:

```
RSpec.describe User do
  describe '#first_name' do
    it 'returns the first name' do
      # test code goes here
    end
  end
end
```

Sometimes I want to test a feature that doesn't have a neat one-to-one relationship with a method. In that case I'll put a description of the feature inside a `describe`.

```
RSpec.describe User do
  describe 'phone format' do
    it 'strips the non-numeric characters' do
      # test code goes here
    end
  end
end
```

12.3.2   When I use context

I tend to use `context` when I want to test various permutations of a behavior.

```
RSpec.describe User do
  describe 'phone format' do
    context 'phone number is not the right length' do
      # test code goes here
    end

    context 'contains non-numeric characters' do
      # test code goes here
    end
  end
end
```

That's all! The `describe`/`context` decision for me is usually a quick and light one, and frankly it's not that consequential, and it doesn't matter too much which one you choose.

12.4   Let, let! and instance variables

RSpec's `let` helper method is a way of defining values that are used in tests. Below is a typical example.

```
RSpec.describe User do
  let(:user) { User.new }

  it 'does not have an id when first instantiated' do
    expect(user.id).to be nil
  end
end
```

Another common way of setting values is to use instance variables in a `before` block like in the following example.

```
RSpec.describe User do
  before { @user = User.new }

  it 'does not have an id when first instantiated' do
    expect(@user.id).to be nil
  end
end
```

There are some differences between the `let` approach and the instance variable approach, with one in particular that's quite significant.

Differences between let and instance variables

First, there's the stylistic difference. The syntax is of course a little different between the two approaches. Instance variables are of course prefixed with @. Some people might prefer one syntax over the other. I personally find the `let` syntax ever so slightly tidier.

There are also a couple mechanical differences. Because of how instance variables work in Ruby, you can use an undefined instance variable and Ruby won't complain. This presents a slight danger. You could for example accidentally pass some undefined instance variable to a method, meaning you'd really be passing `nil` as the argument. This means you might be testing something other than the behavior you meant to test. This danger is admittedly remote though. Nonetheless, the `let` helper defined not an instance variable but a new method (specifically, a *memoized* method—we'll see more on this shortly), meaning that if you typo your method's name, Ruby will most certainly complain, which is of course good.

The other mechanical difference is that `let` can create values that get evaluated lazily. I personally find this to be a dangerous and bad idea, which I'll explain below, but it is a capability that the helper offers.

Perhaps the most important difference between `let` and instance variables is that **instance variables, when set in a `before` block, can leak from one file to another**. If for example an instance variable called @customer is set in "File A", then "File B" can reference @customer and get the value that was set in File A. Obviously this is bad because we want our tests to be completely deterministic and independent of one another.

12.4.1   How let works and the difference between let and let!

I used to assume that `let` simply defines a new variable for me to use. Upon closer inspection, I learned that `let` is a **method that returns a method**. More specifically, `let` returns a *memoized* method, a method that only gets run once.

Since that's perhaps kind of mind-bending, let's take a closer look at what exactly this means.

An example method

Consider this method that 1) prints something and then 2) returns a value.

```
def my_name
  puts 'thinking about what my name is...'
  'Jason Swett'
end

puts my_name
```

When we run `puts my_name`, we see the string that gets printed (`puts 'thinking about what my name is...'`) followed by the value that gets returned by the method (Jason Swett).

```
$ ruby my_name.rb
thinking about what my name is...
Jason Swett
```

Now let's take a look at some `let` syntax that will create the same method.

```
describe 'my_name' do
  let(:my_name) do
    puts 'thinking about what my name is...'
    'Jason Swett'
  end

  it 'returns my name' do
    puts my_name
  end
end
```

When we run this test file and invoke the my_name method, the same exact thing happens: the method putses some text and returns my name.

```
$ rspec my_name_spec.rb
thinking about what my name is...
Jason Swett
.

Finished in 0.00193 seconds (files took 0.08757 seconds to load)
1 example, 0 failures
```

Just to make it blatantly obvious and to prove that my_name is indeed a method call and not a variable reference, here's a version of this file with parentheses after the method call.

```
describe 'my_name' do
  let(:my_name) do
    puts 'thinking about what my name is...'
    'Jason Swett'
  end

  it 'returns my name' do
    puts my_name() # this explicitly shows that my_name() is a method call
  end
end
```

Memoization

Here's a version of the test that calls my_name twice. Even though the method gets called twice, it only actually gets evaluated once.

```
describe 'my_name' do
  let(:my_name) do
    puts 'thinking about what my name is...'
    'Jason Swett'
  end

  it 'returns my name' do
    puts my_name
    puts my_name
  end
end
```

If we run this test, we can see that the return value of my_name gets printed twice and the thinking about what my name is... part only gets printed once.

```
$ rspec my_name_spec.rb
thinking about what my name is...
Jason Swett
Jason Swett

.

Finished in 0.002 seconds (files took 0.08838 seconds to load)
1 example, 0 failures
```

The lazy evaluation of let vs. the immediate evaluation of let!

When we use let, the code inside our block gets evaluated **lazily**. In other words, none of the code inside the block gets evaluated until we actually call the method created by our let block.

Take a look at the following example.

```
describe 'let' do
  let(:message) do
    puts 'let block is running'
    'VALUE'
  end

  it 'does stuff' do
    puts 'start of example'
    puts message
    puts 'end of example'
  end
end
```

When we run this, we'll see start of example first because the code inside our let block doesn't get evaluated until we call the message method.

```
$ rspec let_example_spec.rb
start of example
let block is running
VALUE
end of example

.

Finished in 0.00233 seconds (files took 0.09836 seconds to load)
1 example, 0 failures
```

The "bang" version of let, let!, evaluates the contents of our block immediately, without waiting for the method to get called.

```
describe 'let!' do
  let!(:message) do
```

```
  puts 'let block is running'
  'VALUE'
end

it 'does stuff' do
  puts 'start of example'
  puts message
  puts 'end of example'
end
end
```

When we run this version, we see `let block is running` appearing before `start of example`.

```
$ rspec let_example_spec.rb
let block is running
start of example
VALUE
end of example
.

Finished in 0.00224 seconds (files took 0.09131 seconds to load)
1 example, 0 failures
```

I always use `let!` instead of `let`. I've never encountered a situation where the lazily-evaluated version would be helpful but I have encountered situations where the lazily-evaluated version would be subtly confusing (e.g. a `let` block is saving a record to the database but it's not abundantly clear exactly at what point in the execution sequence the record gets saved). Perhaps there's some performance benefit to allowing the lazy evaluation but in most cases it's probably negligible. Confusion is often more expensive than slowness anyway.

Chapter 13

Capybara's DSL

Capybara uses a DSL (domain-specific language) to abstract away the business of manipulating the browser.

13.1 Navigation

One of the fundamental things you'll need to do in system specs is navigate to various pages. You can do this using Capybara's `visit` method. The `visit` method can take a relative path or a full URL.

```
visit patients_path
visit 'https://www.codewithjason.com'
```

13.2 Clicking links and buttons

Another common need is to click on links, buttons and other elements. To click on a click, use the `click_on` method.

```
click_on 'Home'
```

Sometimes it's not possible or practical to click an element by its text. In these cases you can combine the `find` method with the `click` method.

```
find('.some-link').click
```

13.3 Interacting with forms

Here's how to interact with various types of form elements.

13.3.1   Text inputs

The `fill_in` method takes a selector (i.e. a label, ID or name attribute) as its first argument and a hash with a value as its second argument.

```
fill_in 'Name', with: 'Jason'
```

This is a case where it's perhaps illuminating to include the optional parentheses and braces to make it abundantly clear what's happening.

```
fill_in('Name', { with: 'Jason' })
```

13.3.2   Select inputs

Just like `fill_in`, `select` takes a selector as its first argument and a hash with a value as its second argument.

```
select 'Michigan', from: 'State'

expect(page).to have_select('state_id', selected: 'Michigan')
```

13.3.3   Checkboxes

The `check` method takes just one argument, a selector.

```
check 'I agree'
```

Sometimes, for dynamically-generated lists of checkboxes, clicking a checkbox by its selector is not appropriate for whatever reason. In these cases I like to combine `find` with `click` in order to check the checkbox I want to check.

```
find("input[type=checkbox]", match: :first).click
```

13.3.4   Radio buttons

Just like `check`, `choose` takes a single argument, a selector.

```
choose 'A Radio Button'
```

13.4   Finding content on the page

You can use the `has_content?` method to determine whether a page has a certain piece of content.

```
page.has_content?('Welcome')
```

If it's a CSS selector you're after, you can use the `has_css?` method.

```
page.has_css?('table tr.foo')
```

Chapter 14

Configuring Capybara

As we saw in the last chapter, Capybara is a Ruby library for manipulating browsers. Inevitably at some point you'll want to make changes to certain aspects of your Capybara configuration. In this chapter we'll look at the various components that are involved in Capybara configuration and how to change their configuration settings.

14.1 Drivers

A *driver* is a tool that manipulates a browser the same way a human would. It can effect perform clicks, keystrokes, navigation and so on.

Why do you need to care about drivers? Because there are multiple drivers that can be used with Capybara. They each have different pros and cons, and you might want to use different drivers for different types of tests.

The driver that Capybara uses by default is called *Rack::Test*[1]. The biggest upside of Rack::Test's is that it's fast. Rack::Test's biggest downside is that it doesn't execute JavaScript. For that you'll need a different driver, like, for example, Selenium WebDriver. Selenium WebDriver has the exact opposite pros and cons as Rack::Test: it executes JavaScript but it's relatively slow.

If you want to use Rack::Test, there's nothing you need to do because it's Capybara's default. Selenium, however, requires some configuration.

14.1.1 Configuring Selenium WebDriver

Selenium WebDriver comes with *bindings* for several languages including Ruby. The delivery mechanism for Selenium WebDriver's Ruby binding as a gem called `selenium-webdriver`.

In order to use Selenium WebDriver you'll need to install the `selenium-webdriver` gem.

---

[1] https://github.com/rack/rack-test

```
# Gemfile
gem "selenium-webdriver"
```

Remember that by default Capybara will use the `Rack::Test` driver. If we want Capybara to use a different driver instead (in this case Selenium), we have to tell it so by changing the `Capybara.default_driver` setting.

This can be done in `spec/spec_helper.rb` or in any file that your test environment includes. I personally like to put my Capybara driver configuration in a separate file called, for example, `spec/support/driver.rb`. This way all my Capybara driver configuration can live in one cohesive file, neither cluttering up my main RSpec configuration file nor being cluttered by non-driver configuration details.

```
# spec/support/driver.rb
Capybara.default_driver = :selenium
```

If Selenium WebDriver is set as Capybara's `default_driver`, it will be used for all tests, even ones that don't involve JavaScript. Since Selenium WebDriver is slower than Rack::Test, it's more efficient to let Capybara default to Rack::Test and only use Selenium WebDriver for tests that explicitly need it.

To configure Capybara this way, don't specify a `default_driver`. Instead set only `javascript_driver`.

```
Capybara.javascript_driver = :selenium

RSpec.configure do |config|
  config.before(:each, type: :system) do
    driven_by :selenium_headless
  end
end
```

When Capybara is configured this way, Selenium WebDriver will only be used for tests where `js:   true` is specified, like so:

```
describe "Creating a product", js: true do
```

All other tests will use Capybara's default driver.

14.1.2   Selenium in headless mode

Unlike Rack::Test, running tests with Selenium WebDriver will cause a browser window to open.[2] This means that while tests are running, you can't really do anything else on your machine. A browser window will continually pop into focus

---

[2]The reason Rack::Test doesn't open a browser window is because it doesn't actually use a browser at all. Instead it interacts directly with your application's Rack middleware.

and interrupt whatever you're trying to do. (Your keystrokes and clicks may also accidentally interfere with the tests.) Here's how to configure Selenium WebDriver (specifically, the Chrome flavor) so that it operates *headlessly*—that is, without opening a browser window.

```
# spec/support/driver.rb

Capybara.register_driver :selenium_headless do |app|
  options = Selenium::WebDriver::Chrome::Options.new
  options.add_argument("--headless")

  Capybara::Selenium::Driver.new(
    app,
    browser: :chrome,
    options: options
  )
end

Capybara.javascript_driver = :selenium_headless
```

Configuring Capybara this way has an unfortunate drawback: if you want to watch a test execute in order to troubleshoot it, you can't. For this reason I like to wrap my `javascript_driver` configuration in a check for an environment variable flag.

```
unless ENV["SHOW_BROWSER"].present?
  Capybara.javascript_driver = :selenium_headless
end
```

With a flag like this, you can prepend SHOW_BROWSER=true to your `rspec` commands on the occasions when you want to see a test run in the browser.

```
$ SHOW_BROWSER=true rspec spec/my_system_spec.rb
```

Note that the environment variable name is arbitrary. In this case I happened to choose SHOW_BROWSER but there's nothing special about that name.

14.1.3 Controlling the window size

If a browser window is, for example, too small, then some tests may misbehave because the elements the test interacts with are outside of the viewport. Often you'll need to specify a certain window size in order for the tests to use a normal-sized window.

```
Capybara.register_driver :selenium_headless do |app|
  options = Selenium::WebDriver::Chrome::Options.new
```

```
  options.add_argument("--window-size=1920,1080")

  Capybara::Selenium::Driver.new(
    app,
    browser: :chrome,
    options: options
  )
end

Capybara.javascript_driver = :selenium_headless
```

It's normal in a Rails app to have kind of a lot of Capybara driver configuration. For this reason, I again strongly recommend placing this configuration in a dedicated file rather than allowing the driver configuration to clutter up the `spec/spec_helper.rb` file.

14.2   Networking

For local development it's of course typical to start a Rails server that runs on `localhost:3000`. When Capybara runs, it runs an additional instance of your application on the *Capybara server*. The Capybara server of course can't run on `localhost:3000` because that port would conflict with the development Rails server. For that matter, the Capybara server can't run on any other port that happens to be in use by any other service. It has to be on a unique port.

The way this is handled is that, when the Capybara server starts, it selects an open, unused port on which to run, like 55516 or 55564 for example. (You can see a test run's Capybara server port for yourself if you run a test that opens a browser window and look to the URL bar while the test is running.) If you leave your Capybara networking settings at their defaults, `127.0.0.1` will be used for the Capybara server host, and your URL bar will show something like `http://127.0.0.1:55516`, with the port varying on a run-by-run basis.

14.2.1   server_host and server_port

The `server_host` setting determines the address on which the Capybara server will accept connections. The default is `127.0.0.1`. When the Capybara server needs to be accessed by an outside client, such as when the tests are being run via Docker, for example, and the test browser and Capybara server are in two different containers, the `server_host` will need to be set to accept connections from clients other than `127.0.0.1`. To accept connections from anywhere, `server_host` can be set to `0.0.0.0`.

```
Capybara.server_host = "0.0.0.0"
```

In most normal, non-Dockerized testing scenarios, `server_host` can be left unset since both the test browser and the Capybara server will be living on 127.0.0.1.

14.2.2 app_host

The `app_host` setting tells Capybara the default URL to use when given a relative URL to visit. For example, if `app_host` is set to `http://localhost:3000`, then an instruction to visit `products/1` will result in a request to `http://localhost:3000/products/1`. If `app_host` is set to `https://en.wikipedia.org`, visiting `wiki/The_Beatles` will result in a request to `https://en.wikipedia.org/wiki/The_Beatles`. The `app_host` setting can be set as follows:

```
Capybara.app_host = "http://localhost:5000"
```

The default value for `app_host` is `nil`.

14.3 Wait time

When a test contains a line like `expect(page).to have_content("Success")`, Capybara doesn't immediately give up if it doesn't immediately detect the word "Success" on the page. It will wait a certain period of time before it decides that the expected content isn't there and is never coming. The reason for this is that content of course never loads immediately. Some pages are slow and may take, for example, 800ms to load.

The default amount of time that Capybara will wait is two seconds. If you have pages that are even slower than that, you can adjust the wait time using the following directive:

```
Capybara.default_max_wait_time = 10
```

Alternatively, wait time can be set on a per-test basis by using the `using_wait_time` helper in tests.

```
Capybara.using_wait_time(10) do
  expect(page).to have_content("Success")
end
```

Remember that setting `default_max_wait_time` comes with a cost. In cases where a piece of content is legitimately not present on the page, the test will not fail until the default max wait time has been reached. So if the wait time has been set to 10 seconds, for example, such tests will take no less than 10 seconds to run when they fail. By setting Capybara's wait time on a case-by-case basis, this problem is avoided.

About the author

Jason Swett is a software engineer, consultant, international speaker and host of the Code with Jason Podcast. Jason has many hobbies and interests, including chess, music, robotics, AI, biology, psychology, science, language, culture, sociology, cooking, business, economics and history. He lives in Sand Lake, Michigan with his wife and two sons.